Seeking the Soul

the music of Alfred Schnittke

Compiled by George Odam

Alfred Schnittke in Wien, 1948

4

Seeking the Soul

the music of
Alfred Schnittke

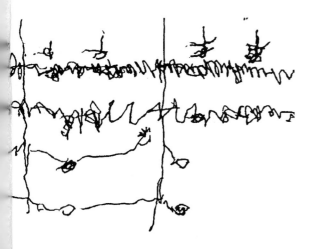

GUILDHALL
School of Music & Drama

On the CD included
with this publication:

1 – 2 Trio

GSMD Music Hall, 10 January 2001:

Moderato

Adagio

Asch Trio:

Roman Mints, violin

Maxim Rysanov, viola

Kristine Blaumane, cello

3 – 5 Viola Concerto

Barbican Hall, 10 May 2000:

Largo

Allegro Molto

Largo

Guildhall Symphony Orchestra

Maxim Rysanov, viola

Takuo Yuasa, conductor

6 Piano Quartet

GSMD Music Hall, 31 May 2001:

Allegro

Asch Trio:

Roman Mints, violin

Maxim Rysanov, viola

Kristine Blaumane, cello

and Vita Panomariovaite, piano

Published in 2002 by:
The Guildhall School of Music & Drama
Barbican
Silk Street
LONDON
EC2Y 8DT
Tel: 020 7628 2571
www.gsmd.ac.uk

ISBN 0 900423 05 6

We gratefully acknowledge the inspiration and assistance of the Centre for Russian Studies at Goldsmiths College, University of London, in the production of this volume, including the many new photographs in the possession of the Director of the Centre, Alexander Ivashkin, which we have been given permission to use.

Advisory Team for the Guildhall School Press:
Dalya Crispin
Peter Gane
Eric Hollis
Alexander Ivashkin
George Odam
Peter Shellard
Alessandro Timossi

Recording engineer: David Foster

Design and typesetting: John Peacock

Printed and bound in Great Britain by
Antony Rowe Ltd, Chippenham, Wiltshire

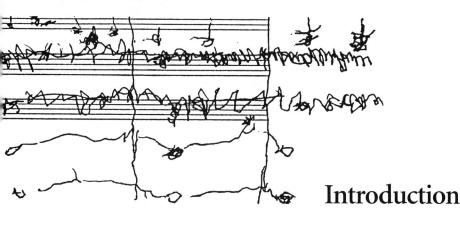

Introduction

Alexander Ivashkin

Alfred Schnittke (1934–98) needs very little introduction. During the latter part of the twentieth century his music was performed thousands of times all around the world. Schnittke's works have been recorded on more than 100 compact discs released by various companies. His major compositions – nine symphonies, three operas, ballets, numerous concertos, concerti grossi, sonatas for different instruments – have been heard all over the world.

In Schnittke's music we find a mixture of old and new styles, of modern, post-modern, classical and baroque ideas. It reflects a very complex, peculiar and fragile mentality of the late twentieth century. Like Shostakovich or Mahler, Schnittke presents more than just musical ideas: there is always something symbolic in his musical language, which leads us to the 'genetic well' of a memory of past generations. Schnittke's music speaks a universal language with 'roots' clear to everybody.

I met Alfred Schnittke in the late 1960s – the short period of Khrushchev's thaw – when Alfred was beginning to become very famous in both Russia and the West. His music was included in the programmes of a number of different modern music festivals. In 1969 Schnittke started to work on his First Symphony; five years later it was performed in Gorky – a city closed to foreigners, 400 kilometres north-east of Moscow. The communist officials did not allow this work to be performed in Moscow, as the music seemed to them much too dissident. Elements of collage in this music and its theatricality also shocked many purists, so much so that the First Symphony was performed only once in the following decade. The response of the public however, was enthusiastic: since then, each new composition by Schnittke has been eagerly awaited.

Later on, Schnittke changed his attitude to the direct quotation. He was looking for a universal language that could combine different stylistic elements, but not necessarily direct quotation. The hidden, extra-musical energy emerges in clashes of completely different styles, different languages, even different musics. The material of Schnittke's music is often drawn from the 'genetic well' of cultural memory. He told me once: 'I am just fixing what I hear ... It's not me who writes my music, I am just a tool, a bearer'.

5

Alfred Schnittke, Prague, 1978

For many years Alfred Schnittke was not allowed to attend performances of his works in the West. In the Soviet Union, one needed to obtain a so-called 'exit visa' to be able to go abroad. This small stamp used to be a great privilege for those who behaved in accordance to the official rules of the Soviet Empire. One usually got this stamp just few hours before departure – it was a favourite 'strategy' of the Soviet composers' officials in order to be able to cancel any trip just at a few hours' notice, if necessary. Until he was 43, Schnittke could travel only to Eastern European countries – and infrequently, even then. Most often letters of invitations sent to Schnittke care of the Soviet Composers' Union disappeared into a drawer of the Union's boss, Tikhon Khrennikov, and remained unanswered.

Schnittke did not make his first trip to the West as an adult until 1977 – but it was not as a composer. He performed a harpsichord/piano part in his own Concerto Grosso No. 1 with the Lithuanian Chamber Orchestra under Saulus Sondeckis. Several concerts in Austria also brought him back to Vienna, where he had spent three years in the 1940s and where he had started his musical lessons.

1985 was a climactic year in Schnittke's life. He had just turned 50. Several masterpieces had been finished and premiered that year, including the Concerto for Mixed Choir, the ⊙ *Concerto for Viola and Orchestra*, the Concerto Grosso No. 3, the ⊙ *String Trio*, and '(K)ein Sommernachtstraum' for orchestra. It was the year of the first performance of his ballet 'Sketches' at the prestigious Bolshoi Theatre in Moscow. Schnittke also finished his orchestra piece 'Ritual' and started his Cello Concerto No. 1, but was unable to complete it: on 21 July 1985 he suffered a major stroke, his first, which was so severe that he was clinically dead for some ten minutes before he was resuscitated.

'Although I don't have any Russian blood', Schnittke said, 'I am tied to Russia, having spent all my life here. On the other hand, much of what I've written is somehow related to German music and to the logic which comes out of being German, although I did not specially want this ... Like my German forefathers, I live in Russia, I can speak and write Russian far better than German. But I am not Russian ... My Jewish half gives me no peace: I know none of the three Jewish languages – but I look like a typical Jew.'

⊙ The *Concerto for Viola and Orchestra* and the *String Trio* are on the included CD, tracks 3–5 and 1–2

Schnittke was one of the most prolific composers in the twentieth century. His works are considered an established part of the standard instrumental repertoire for orchestras, chamber groups and soloists. In the 1970s–1980s Schnittke was enjoying enormous, unusual popularity in Russia. 'His music used to be our language, more perfect that the spoken one' as one Russian critic said. Concert promoters used to call the police to prevent halls from overcrowding and the chaos that ensued when Schnittke's music was performed in Moscow, Leningrad or Novosibirsk. All the performances of Schnittke's music were important events for Soviet listeners: in Schnittke's music they could find metaphysical ideas and spiritual values, absent in real life during the endless years of 'terror', 'thaw', 'cold war', or 'stagnation'. In the 1980s–1990s Schnittke's music was performed extensively everywhere in the West, from Germany and USA to South America and New Zealand, to great acclaim.

After 1991 Schnittke lived in Hamburg, coming to Moscow only occasionally. Surprisingly, he wrote more than half of his major compositions during his last thirteen years, when he was gravely ill. One of his last works, the Ninth Symphony (1996–7), the composer wrote with his left hand, when he was already unable to speak and could hardly move. In the same period, between 1996 and 1998, he also completed a piece for viola and chamber orchestra and a set of variations for string quartet.

After his first stroke in 1985, Schnittke fought the effects of his illness until 3 August 1998, when he died in Hamburg of a fifth stroke. Schnittke's funeral in Moscow on 10 August 1998, attended by thousands of peo-ple, was a tribute of honour and admiration to the greatest Russian composer since Shostakovich. 'The last genius of the twentieth century' he was called by all the Russian news-papers and, quite belatedly, Russian officials.

Seeking the Soul is the first-ever attempt in the West to present a collection of scholarly writings on Schnittke. This collection is based on a two-day international conference organised in January 2001 by the Guildhall School of Music & Drama in collaboration with the Centre for Russian Music/Schnittke Archive at Goldsmiths College, University of London and the BBC.

I am very happy to introduce some distinguished international specialists on Schnittke, who are presented in this volume. Valentina Kholopova, Professor at the Moscow

Alfred Schnittke, at home in Moscow, 1984

Alfred Schnittke, at home in Moscow, 1978

Conservatory, published the first-ever book on Schnittke's music in Russia in 1990. She is a well-known analyst of Schnittke's works with numerous international publications to her credit. Georg Borchardt, President of the 'Gustav Mahler Society' in Germany, presents his paper on 'Mahler and Schnittke'. Dr Maria Kostakeva, originally from Bulgaria, lives and teaches in Bochum, Germany. She is very active as a writer in the field of contemporary music. Ronald Weitzman is the leading reviewer for *Tempo* magazine, and he has published excellent reports on the latest premières of Schnittke's operas *Gesualdo* and *History of Dr Faust* in Vienna and in Hamburg respectively. Weitzman's paper deals with an interesting issue of 'shadow sound': hidden meaning in Schnittke's music.

We are delighted also to present three papers written by young musicians. Maria Krivenski, a lecturer in piano at Goldsmiths College, investigates the evolution of piano style of the composer – from his very early works in the 1960s up to his last compositions written in 1993. Paul Westwood, a student at the Guildhall, discusses some structural issues in Schnittke's chamber music. Fiona Héarún-Javakhishvili (a postgraduate student at the Centre for Russian Music, Goldsmiths College) presents her concept of Schnittke's early style in his Sonata for Violin and Piano No. 1.

ALEXANDER IVASHKIN is one of three cellists (along with Mstislav Rostropovich and Natalia Gutman) for whom Schnittke wrote his cello works. Ivashkin recorded the Schnittke complete cello works on the Chandos label. A close friend of the composer, he has published several books on Schnittke, including the only book on Schnittke and his music in English (*Alfred Schnittke*, London, 1996), as well as *Schnittke* (Torino, 1993), *Conversations with Alfred Schnittke* (Moscow, 1994), *Alfred Schnittke über das Leben und die Musik* (Munich, 1998), *Schnittke Reader* (Indiana UP, 2002, forthcoming).

Schnittke and shadow-sounds

Ronald Weitzman

'Shadow-sounds', or in German *Schattenklänge*, is one of numerous words Schnittke invented. He spoke with his family, and indeed continued often to think, in a German strange to most of today's native-speaking Germans. These compound nouns of his own making have an impact of unanticipated significance. Those of us brought up in countries where English is the spoken language rarely hear about *Schattenkläng*, *Klangschatten*, the sound of shadows. Such terms haven't become attached to the mere mention of Schnittke's name as has another designation he coined, to wit, 'polystylism'. Yet I consider 'shadow-sounds' an important symbol, and certainly less misleading than the term 'polystylism', which easily becomes a meaningless label – or just a designation used when referring to Schnittke's encyclopaedic absorption of a multitude of musical styles – but which, as distinct from the composer's actual quoting from other sources, Alexander Ivashkin more correctly describes as a 'genetic view' of memories.

Based on a transcript of a talk given at the Seeking the Soul Schnittke Festival, Barbican Arts and Guildhall School of Music & Drama, London, January 2001

By 1984 – a year before the composer suffered his first stroke – shadow-sounds are burrowing beneath the very membrane of Schnittke's music. As part and parcel of his 'sound-world' they elongate the spiralling sense of space that his music inhabits. But long before 1984, the sound of shadows represents not only a particular sound-quality that we find in Schnittke's music, it also characterises an ethos central to what Schnittke, the man and the musician, is about. While many seek to explore the many contradictions in Schnittke, I, in contrast, will strongly contest that man and musician in Schnittke are incapable of being separated without inestimable harm being done to one or to the other. This principle sets apart the *great* artist from the *clever* artist, and needs stating – or should I say re-stating – as many members of today's critical fraternity, when they aren't ignoring the principle, tend to denigrate it.

Let me say straight away that Schnittke's first twin masterworks carry no obvious polystylistic features. I refer, firstly, to the Piano Quintet, over which the composer agonised for more than four years, and, secondly, to his Requiem, which by contrast emerged painlessly from material Schnittke had discarded from the Quintet. In the Quintet's closing movement, the unvarying presence of a repeated passacaglia and a waltz based on the notes spelling out Bach's name passes through the shadow of the Dies Irae theme, before the music fades into a world our senses are unable to perceive. Schnittke had wanted to write a small *instrumental* requiem movement within his Quintet; this wouldn't work, as the themes he conceived were simply not instrumental. So, this 'shadow-work of unrealised ideas', became a choral Requiem – an offshoot of the Quintet, and quite independent of it. And as to a public performance of the Requiem: well, the Soviet authorities forbad the playing of liturgical music of any kind, so Schnittke brought into play another form of shadowing. He snugly tucked the Requiem away *within* a stage production in Moscow of Schiller's drama *Don Carlos*, the Requiem being performed as a part of the play itself – a mass being sung *behind* the scenery.

The idea of 'shadowing' emerged in a different way when the BBC Symphony Orchestra, then under the music directorship of Gennady Rozhdestvensky, commissioned a new work from Schnittke. As Schnittke's long-time champion, Rozhdestvensky suggested his friend commemorate the Austrian composer Anton Bruckner. Schnittke had, in 1977, visited St Florian, the collegiate church in Linz where Bruckner had been organist and where Bruckner's remains now lie. On that occasion, Schnittke had heard evening mass being sung by a choir. But the sound was coming from a place hidden from view. His Second Symphony became a setting of the Catholic mass. But it's what Schnittke calls an 'invisible mass' – the choir sounding strangely remote behind a symphonic edifice. From the mid- to the late 1970s, Schnittke, like other composers working in the torpid Brezhnev era, had to find ways of getting round absurd Soviet strictures. And Schnittke's genius is that, by way of the ingenuity he showed in the overcoming of stifling obstacles, he began to produce original works of art wherein the seed-bed of shadow-sounds were being sown.

It was in the Soviet film studio, largely free from prying official eyes, and which he came to use much like a scientist uses a research laboratory, that Schnittke contrived, explored and began to advance within his own music shadow-sounds. For the purpose of this chapter, I'll jump to the year 1979, the year a friend of Schnittke's – the film director Larissa Shepitko – died in a car crash. She had been working on a film called 'Farewell to Matyora', which her husband Elem Klimov, also a director, took over after her death. Schnittke collaborated on the film score with three other composers, who included Sofia Gubaidulina and Victor Suslin; but it was Schnittke who explored the idea of using a chorus. One essential idea of the film was that is was to come to an end – yet, instead of ending, the film opened out onto a larger world. Seeking to portray this musically, Schnittke hit upon the idea of applying a choir and orchestra.

> What I had hoped for didn't come about: everything suddenly, as it were, ceased – nothing was. And so I searched for something else … The choir sang, very gently, echoes of well-known choral works, like Beethoven's *Missa Solemnis* and specially old Russian church music, which is always unaccompanied. It came to shadow-sounds. These shadows extend the sound dimension; one perceives a second boundary lying behind the first, suspects a third perimeter, then a fourth, and so on. This opened up a new, illusory sound-space. One does not hear these shadow-sounds – and yet, no, one *does* hear them, but so faintly as to be barely audible. We don't perceive them consciously but we listen in on them unawares. Most people, supposing they comprehend music, don't know at all how this impression arises. What sort of sound it is nobody can say! But shadow-sounds there are, and they do make a difference.

Significantly, Schnittke was already eschewing the writing of illustrative music expected from, indeed required by, composers of film scores. Alongside the birth and growth of the sounds of shadows we find Schnittke applying what amounts to a splitting off of a musical idea from what *appears* to be happening out there in the visual world. The film 'Agony' about Rasputin, dating from 1974, is particularly important in this respect – and its controlling repetitive theme would dominate the last movement of Schnittke's Second Cello Concerto written sixteen years later.

In the Fourth Symphony, splitting off, deliberate non-synchronisation, becomes fully manifest and fundamental to the musical plan. Here, emerging from and, at the same time, yoked to a ground bass represented by the semitone interval of Jewish cantorial music there flows from this Jewish source three great Christian tributaries – the Catholic (represented by the minor part of a tetrachord), the Orthodox (represented by the minor mode within the tetrachord) and the Lutheran (represented by two ascending tritones). In the Fourth Symphony one may concentrate on what's *behind* the tolling bells, as strands spill over each other. It is an early instance of non-synchronicity applied in Schnittke's music. When, at the very end of the Fourth Symphony, the strands come together in diatonic harmony, basses sing the Ave Maria – though, again Schnittke hid this fact until he went to live in Germany; in early performances, the bass line was wordlessly vocalised.

All of this paves the way for the most important of Schnittke's works, where shadow-sounds intertwine and are deliberately staggered, so ensuring that any coinciding, any synchronisation is side-stepped. I refer to his ballet *Peer Gynt*. Schnittke worked together with the American-born choreographer John Neumeier, whose ballet company in Hamburg has built up a unique reputation over the last thirty years or so of the twentieth century. Choreographer and composer agreed at the outset that two unparalleled themes should unfold simultaneously. Schnittke resolutely discarded the norm that ballet music should accompany the dance, and Neumeier's special talent is his refusal to choreograph note for note. As Schnittke has said in interview:

> [With Neumeier] music and dance remain two dimensions, the music being the shadow of the movement, and at the same time the movement being the shadow of the music. Now, when [every detail of what's happening on stage is out of step with what's going on in the music], a consciousness of the music arises that stands independently – perception extends itself. One now senses, sees and hears – two worlds. This peculiar feeling of the non-synchronicity of the two processes [operating independently of each other] is for me very important.

Neumeier's narrative follows Peer Gynt, as he is born – with seven personalities – then as he grows up in his native Norway, and abducts Ingrid on her wedding day; again as he ventures Out Into the World – Neumeier here substitutes Ibsen's dispatch of Peer to Africa by sending his Peer off into the illusory world of Hollywood and super-stardom. Following his descent into lunacy, Peer returns to Norway, a broken nobody. Finally, a vast epilogue reveals what Ibsen's epic only hints at: a world *apart from* this world. Central to this imagined world are Peer and Solveig, Solveig being the eternal, idealised woman who stands ever by Peer's side. Schnittke's music unfolds symphonically, on a level independent of Neumeier's choreography. Themes associated with Peer, and the sway of the feminine over his very being, intertwine, spiral-like. Schnittke refers to the four zones of *Peer Gynt* not as sections but as *Kreise*, the German word for circles or, more accurately in this context, open-ended spheres. Boundaries are thus crossed, they overlap; for a *Kreis*, a sphere, is a circle, and a circle by definition has no top, no bottom. Everything that has happened in Acts 1, 2 and 3, where themes have been added, one by one, come together in this extraordinary 25-minute epilogue. We have heard all the themes – and yet, as they enmesh, so are the themes transformed – and our notion of both space and time appears to be drawn out.

Above, I referred to Schnittke using a choir in the film 'Farewell to Matyora'. Schnittke experimented with this idea in another film. And then, as he was thinking about the fourth, imaginary 'sphere' in *Peer Gynt*, he knew that somehow he would require there to be a choir here also. He solved the technical problem of what is an unbroken passacaglia – it's also the only new theme running through the epilogue. Thus an unending sound-perspective opens up. Schnittke speaks of the epilogue as follows: 'The permanent reinstatement of earlier themes and the constant joining of newer musical material were the leading principles for the whole composition. The entire music of the ballet is like a preliminary stage to this fourth and last "sphere".'

Neumeier tells me that, in his mind, Peer and Solveig have been through purgatory just before the epilogue. Diverging from this, Schnittke makes it clear it is just such a purgatorial world that this endless Adagio inhabits. So here's another instance where there's a deliberate lack of coinciding, both from within the music and outside it, shadow-sounds thus shifting our apprehension of what is happening. The orchestral texture is important to the music's restless, ambiguous pulse and underlying tension, as we become sort of conscious of the filtered sound, like an elongated shadow, of the taped choir.

To hear what is inaudible, to realise another world that is not of this world, is an impossibility. The philosopher Immanuel Kant put a convincing stop to that kind of metaphysical speculation. Yet that *aim* is central to so much of what Schnittke is about. His music is hovering between two worlds. Well do I recall how Alfred fixed his eyes on me during a rehearsal, beseeching me: did *I* at least grasp what he was failing to instil into the imagination of a not very comprehending solo violinist? 'I am in total earnest!' he implored, when, in the score of the Fourth Violin Concerto, the soloist is instructed *not* to touch the strings with the bow. By the time he came to write the ⊙ *String Trio*, the ⊙ *Viola Concerto* and, above all, *Peer Gynt*, the inaudible has given way to the sound of shadows permeating the musical fabric.

There's an ostensible, unnerving dualism in Schnittke's music – the earthly *versus* the spiritual, bent on exposing the tawdriness, the diabolical

⊙ The *String Trio* and the *Viola Concerto* are on the included CD, tracks 1–2 and 3–5

13

side, of the worldly – and it's precisely this compelling force which we, the listeners, while responding with all our nerve-strands and emotions, need fully to acknowledge, albeit with caution. As we read in St Peter's First Letter – words Schnittke chose to head his *Faust* Cantata – 'Be sober-minded, be watchful; for your enemy, the Devil, roams about like a roaring lion, looking for a victim to devour.' Schnittke's music, at its best, is a distillation of an unbearable tension of being, of existence. It carries with it a severe health warning. Yet I believe we are required to find within ourselves a mettle, a stamina, to take that load, that burden, upon our own shoulders if we are to begin to understand him: without this, you deny his music its elemental importance, and hear instead only hysteria.

Schnittke is subtle and deep. Don't be deceived by his apparent *naïveté*. He knows exactly what he's referring to when he speaks of 'the Devil leading me by the nose'. Elsewhere he has said: 'I know that the Devil is immanent and that one cannot get rid of him by immersing oneself in something pure – [for] there, too, the Devil is present!' He speaks articulately about times in history, and above all about the time he lived in, when the devil came down to earth, baring his teeth. We have his undisputed testimony about this. Schnittke knew the limitations of the empirical approach – and if he goes overboard in his distrust of the rational, that distrust is spurred on by his unrelentingly fierce perception of multitudes of people being transfixed by 'the mimicry, the gesture, the entire bearing' of the demagogue, whether this devil-come-down-to-earth be, say, a Stalin or a Hitler. This, he says, is

> the eternal demonic figure that is always reappearing ... That is precisely the Devil at work. Millions but millions of human beings participate in the satanic theatre, for years they are hoodwinked ... It is inconceivable that such a thing was still possible after the nineteenth century, after the apparent victory of humanism [and reason]. [But] All at once this darkness [descended], a darkness more dreadful than the whole history of mankind.

And in his *Faust* Cantata, which became the last act of his opera *The History of Dr Johann Faustus*, Schnittke gives further expression of the crucial importance of 'not closing one's eyes to satanic elements but [dealing] with them by facing them'. The opera so far has only been performed in a much truncated version where more than an hour of music is missing and in which the order of events is as the conductor and the director decide, not as the composer wrote them down. 'The diabolical world must be unfathomable when gazed upon,' Schnittke says in interview with Hannelore

14

Gerlach, 'and must likewise so remain! I made up my mind to do [*Faust*] in a way it hadn't been approached before … I adhere only to the [original 1587] *Volksbuch*, and no other, [as representation of the Middle Ages is] a false Middle Ages.'

(And I remind you that one of Schnittke's many shorter works where the 'fake' takes precedence is his sort of humorous *Not a [Mid]Summernight's Dream*.) When Schnittke is writing in an illusory antiquity, we have a further instance that's allied to the shadow world. When speaking of *Faust*, on which he worked on and off for two decades, Schnittke has warned of what he calls 'the excessive rationalisation of the machine'. He adds, 'one is not doing justice to his very existence. When referring to the diabolical world, one must deny the rational principle … I should like to respect it as something spontaneous, where everything unexpected or unforeseen happens … The irrational does not lie beyond the rational mind, it just cannot be deciphered by it.' And he goes on to say,

> One can give music a certain illusory dependence on time, as e.g., the way Arvo Pärt has written for years. It's music that originates in a quasi sixteenth century, but actually there never was such music then. It now appears as if it were old music: I repeat: it appears so. But it is composed today. And what I'm now writing in Faust will have nothing in common with Pärt's music [which] I love and revere.

Faust and Peer Gynt were the two themes closest to Schnittke's heart. In his last completed symphony, No. 8, where everything is submerged in shadow-sounds, Schnittke's music is as if peering down from some distant vantage-point; as if all illusion, of what he does in a very different way in his great choral works; the expression of one whose searing Christian faith takes on board what John Keats called 'all disagreeables'; music reflecting St Paul's words touch upon what's going on in this stark, intangible, other-worldly score.

In *Gesualdo*, my favourite Schnittke opera, the tormented, self-lacerating madrigalist who murders both his wife and her lover, and who's under the lash of obeying family honour, admits at the height of his unhappiness that, 'were it not for music, loneliness would soon gnaw my soul away, and from its decay bitterness would pour onto my lips from inside me as it dies.' In an incredibly poignant passage, Gesualdo's music passes through the shadow of Amfortas's unending suffering; and the opera begins and finishes with Schnittke composing madrigals of his own. Richard Bletschacher's admirable libretto ends with these words:

Within your walls grows lamenting music, and [the] singing throats crane upwards towards the stars. In vain the tormented brows strain for a reply. He who is alone must take sustenance from the echo of his own cries, his implacably bleeding wounds uncomforted.

This labour which I begin with certain faith and in your name
You will complete, so that the songs will serve to heal the wound of body and soul.
And when my humble creation will, with your holy blessing, be completed,
Then let the Spirit of the Lord be one with my modest inspiration.
I beseech you: Do not extinguish the spark you have lit in me,
Do not abandon the spirit which is mine;
But receive again and again the song of praise from this, your servant.
Amen.

Artistic individuality in Schnittke's overture and his new political mythology

Maria Kostakeva

In 1989 Alfred Schnittke moved from Moscow to Germany. Nine years later, on 3 August 1998, the life of this important figure of contemporary music came to an end. On 10 August 1998, the funeral ceremony took place in a Russian Orthodox Church and he was buried next to some of the most celebrated Russian artists in the cemetery of the Novodevicij Monastery. This brings up some questions: Why did such a famous composer, who had enjoyed freedom and glories in the West, want to be buried in his own country? How could someone who had no drop of Russian blood recognise Russia as his native country? Schnittke had had to learn to live as an alien everywhere. In Russia he was called a Jew and a German; in Germany he was also a foreigner, born in Russia and well known as a Russian composer; he was a Jew who could not speak his own language; and he was a German who had lived in the Soviet Zone. For his whole life, Schnittke was a 'homeless cosmopolitan', as the Russians called the Soviet Jews. This tormented him until he realised that there was no solution to the problem; rescue would not be possible.

If we try to find a key to his secret writing – hidden monograms, symbols, numeral proportions – we discover the real home of this 'homeless cosmopolitan': that undetermined, unconditional, spiritual country; a free space, where art and life, music and its history, political actuality and mythic eternity meet. Schnittke searches for answers to the fundamental question of identity at all levels – national, religious, socio-political, cultural and existential – with his polystylistic method (which he also calls 'stylistic polyphony'). The idea of bringing different epochs face to face in one work, an idea very important to Schnittke, results in a permanent and never-ending process. The polystylistic method is not only an important medium for interpreting the world, but also an instrument for creating a

Based on a transcript of a talk given at the Seeking the Soul Schnittke Festival, Barbican Arts and Guildhall School of Music & Drama, London, January 2001

17

new reality. This peculiar 'Music-Babylon' reflects not only the simultaneity of global reality, but also the image of the human being. In Schnittke's music diverse historical layers (Baroque, Renaissance, Romantic), various church musics (Orthodox, Protestant, Catholic, Jewish), cultural (classical and popular music) and non-cultural phenomena (such as the chaotic environment) are confronted. His music reminds us of Eco's postmodern idea that books all tell us about other books, and that every story retells another story that has already been told long ago.

Schnittke conceived his polystylistic method not as collage and montage of quotations (as with B.A. Zimmermann), but as the simultaneous presence of diverse music languages and time-spaces. Syntactic unities arise that are connected with the music vocabulary of a whole epoch or even a whole culture (such as in the First Symphony). Schnittke feels that a specific system of 'stylistic modulation' comes into being, which has not yet been properly investigated (Schnittke 1994a: 145).

It is a kind of intertextuality: the 'systematical modulation' of text (music) results in innumerable new texts (kinds of music). His Concerto Grosso No. 3 (1985) was written to commemorate the birth anniversaries of five composers (Schütz, Bach, Handel, Scarlatti, Berg). Schnittke explains that the work begins in a neo-classical mood, but after a few minutes the 'museum' explodes: a fragment of the past is confronted with its dangerous and unsure future. The confrontation between this ideally musical 'museum' and the dangerous present determines all of Schnittke's oeuvre. He believes, on the one hand, that the world is perfectly organised by a higher power; on the other hand it seems to him to be a chaotic and multifarious entity, which cannot be arranged or explained. That is why his music brings an apocalyptic meaning into the idyllic colour of stylised old epochs. Two realities are assimilated – the first is a perceptible reality, very strongly constructed by the composer; the other is a virtual reality that comes into being like a reflected face, a phantom, an illusion. There is a paradoxical exchange between the musical and non-musical factors; these non-musical factors take the leading role until they become integrated into the musical flux and eventually dictate the form. Schnittke called his First Symphony 'Symphony-Antisymphony, Antisymphony-Symphony'. As Alexander Ivashkin says:

> In fact, he made an attempt to develop the symphony into a new artefact, one which exists on the border between reality and cultural history and on the border between different types of culture and music, to the point where anything 'artistic' simply emerges from the raw material of everyday life. (Ivashkin 1996: 118)

Apart from his polystylistic method, Schnittke connects to tradition in two ways: through quotation or allusion. While the first principle shows the opposition between 'his own' and 'alien', the second adapts 'the foreign body' and recognises the alien as his own. Thus a foreign text can enter into a dialogue or polemic with a context of his own, or it can be integrated by its own stylistic peculiarities into the work. The alien material (quotation or allusion) seems often to be a strange oasis on the other side of reality. This non-reality can appear like a dream (for example the Mahler quotation in the Fourth Concerto Grosso or Fifth Symphony), like a passing thought in the turbulent musical flow (the Tchaikovsky quotation in the third movement of the First Concerto Grosso), it can be peaceful and harmonious (the Bach allusion and the Christmas song 'Silent Night' in the Second Concerto Grosso), or it can have a demolishing and subversive effect (for example, the whole field of banal popular music in the opera *Faust* and the *Faust Cantata*, or the revolution songs in the opera *Life With an Idiot*).

At the centre of this variegated musical universe stands the opposition between good and evil, which is of great importance in Schnittke's oeuvre. This opposition arises, in his opinion, when good is destroyed by evil. In every one of Schnittke's works, we can observe this confrontation, which manifests itself through different thematic layers appearing often simultaneously. The evil is mostly symbolised by popular culture (*U-Musik*). Schnittke considered the popular tune to be a metaphor for evil, because its uniformity seemed to him indicative of the stagnant, sedentary crowd. He believed that popular culture in a totalitarian regime is an instrument intended to destroy individuality and manipulate the taste of the masses. Trivial music is a sign of provincialism, of narrowness of mind. It is dangerous not only because it is a symbol of stereotypes, of clichés, but also because it can reproduce itself again and again.[1]

Trivial music had been very important in Schnittke's work since the time of his First Symphony (1969–72) and his First Concerto Grosso (1977). The composer described this concept, as in the First Concerto Grosso (1977), thus: 'The banality of the surroundings exerts its disturbing and destroying influence. It interrupts all kind of development and it triumphs at the end' (Schnittke 1994b: 100; my translation). The revealing of negative emotions – broken texture, torn melody, which symbolised the condition of neuroses – is the expression of evil, but not of absolute evil. It is the defeated good. 'The lacerated soul can be good, but it is injured and therefore it is becoming evil' (Ivashkin 1996: 155–6). Trivial music in Schnittke's opinion is a kind of seduction, a kind of evil. For example, the spectacular Tango from

1. Schnittke's ideas regarding the relationship between pop culture and evil are valid not only for a totalitarian system but also for post-industrial society as a whole. A very significant example is the American pop star Marilyn Manson, who identifies himself with the Antichrist. Putting on the mask of the Devil, he sings about a dead God, dead emotions and dead societies ('The liberation rockers from yesterday are the monstrous rockers of today; the satanists of today are the enlightener of tomorrow…' Gross 2000: 50).

the fifth movement, Rondo, in the First Concerto Grosso is similar to the baroque–romantic theme at the beginning of the same part in the Concerto (see Examples 2.1b and 2.1a). Also, in the First Symphony, there is a trivial melody that is related to the Dies Irae. 'I take two notes of this Dies Irae, which are by coincidence identical to the popular tune, and it all turns into triviality – which in this case is not wrong, because there are connections between the Dies Irae and the Devil's banality' (Schnittke 1994c: 86).

2.1a Schnittke, Concerto Grosso No. 1, Part V, Rondo

2.1b Schnittke, Concerto Grosso No. 1, Part V, Rondo

Whereas the sphere of evil and the Devil is revealed through trivial music from the field of Soviet mass culture, the sphere of goodness is expressed through the language of baroque, classical–romantic and expressionistic music, on the one hand, and the liturgical traditions of different religions, on the other hand (see Examples 2.2a and 2.2b: the prologue from *Life with an Idiot*, and Bach's *St Matthew Passion*). The semantics of the 'good–evil' opposition that Schnittke creates include all levels of musical language and forms (stability–instability, constructed–not constructed, tonal–chromatic, melodic entity–nuclear elements, etc.). We can perceive this dichotomy also

20

through the nature of the sounds in his orchestration. In this complex flow all sound categories are integrated; there is no difference between timbre and harmony or between rhythm and intensity. In Schnittke's perception, the loud, sharp and cutting sound lies within the field of evil. This kind of sound, which suggests a catastrophe, can evoke only disquiet, anxiety and horror: what the sound is trying to achieve is in this case nothing more than the portrayal of the disintegration caused by destruction.

While the metallic, harsh sound of brass instruments and percussion reveals the essence of evil, the string and wind instruments are a symbol of the dreaming, broken and hesitant soul. Orchestral sound can suggest also another, very specific sphere in Schnittke's music: the sphere of death and the 'other world'. As Schnittke was ill for a long time and suffered greatly, he was used to living simultaneously in this and the other 'reality'; to be at the same time 'here' and 'there'. The ghostly, shadowy atmosphere of reality on 'the other side' is revealed through the combination of such instruments as the harp, vibraphone, celesta, flexatone, electric guitar, bells or through the use of prepared and amplified piano (for example in the First Concerto

2.2a Schnittke, *Life with an Idiot*, Prologue

21

2.2b Bach, St Matthew Passion, bars 1–2

Grosso). This unreal atmosphere often appears at the end of his works (such as the strange funeral waltz, played by trumpet, trombone and percussion in the final of his Seventh Symphony). A very impressive example is the finale of his ballet *Peer Gynt* – the seemingly endless adagio carries the action away into another dimension, where there will be no more suffering. This specific circular shape without clear contours is like a spiral, coming from nowhere and going into nowhere.

The interplay between good and evil, human and Devil finds its expression in two very important works for the music theatre: in his above-mentioned ballet and in his opera *Faust*. The Devil – whether he is called Mephisto or the Bøyg – does not appear of his own will but because his shady services are needed. The more the character wants to achieve, the more he gets entangled in the Devil's net. The lucid moment comes only with the realisation that there is no way back: that is the theme of *Faust* and *Peer Gynt*. Two worlds are confronted in the ballet: the mythic Norwegian world, the native country of the protagonist, and the world of Hollywood, a world of consuming ambitions and craziness. On the one hand, there is the sphere of Peer – the dreamer, the visionary, the fiancée-abductor, the slave-dealer, the emperor of the world, the madman – on the other hand, the sphere of the mechanical, schizophrenic, heartless film industry. (In Schnittke's and Neumeier's concept there is a connection between the New and the Devil.) The composer believes that the most terrible and brutal events in the history of the human race are always connected with the New. The Devil wants to have everything that is new for himself; he has aspirations and ambitions for experience in unknown fields into which he has not previously entered. The never-ending wanderings of Peer are archetypically connected with Odysseus – but while Odysseus's wanderings lead to his purification and to his return home, the wanderings of Peer and his metamorphosis are revealed as different stations of the Devil's temptation. In his confrontation with life Peer becomes a world citizen, Everybody and at last Nobody. The dialectics between an endless search and return to himself, the problem of loneliness, the striving for identity, all this is enclosed in the mysterious circle of Bøyg. That is the hidden, unknowable nature of things, which is symbolised in the ring in Ibsen's play. Peer cannot break through this circle, because it is the result of his committed sins.

The motive of Bøyg is at the heart of Schnittke's ballet: a chromatic nucleus of three notes, which are played by the gong (Example 2.3). In this way, the invisible presence of Bøyg comes into being not as a melodic shape, but much more through its rhythmic articulation. The nucleus sinks down in a muted cluster of harp and cembalo, which reveals the sorrowful sound of a funeral knell. The strange orchestral sound (to which is added the gong as well as the harp, marimba, cembalo and flexatone) and the contrast between extremely deep and high registers results in an odd dimension, which can be perceived throughout the ballet.

2.3 Schnittke, Peer Gynt

The uncanny cause–effect connection binds Peer with the Bøyg and shows his 'shadow' projection through the gong-motif and its endless reflections. The Bøyg, similar to the Sphinx in Sophocles's *Oedipus rex*, knows the secret of Peer's sinful past and therefore he keeps his fate in his hand. While the mythic Sphinx symbolised neutral trust, which is inaccessible because of Oedipus's tragic ignorance, the Bøyg is much more similar to Mephisto. He is always changing his personae in Ibsen's play: the Man, the Strange Passenger, the Button-Moulder, and the Thin Man. As Peer's life comes to an end, the Button-Moulder, according to the Devil's pact, claims his soul. He insists on evidence of Peer's identity. But as Peer is not able to prove who he is, and as his sin doesn't reach demoniac dimensions, he is not allowed to go to Hell. The catharsis comes only when Solveig can identify him with her love.

There is a parallel pact with the Devil in the opera *Faust*. Led by his intention to penetrate into the intricate era of the sixteenth century, Schnittke had been confronted by the deeply existential problem of the modern epoch: destruction and distortion of the individual as a result of moral disorientation. The action of the opera, based on a medieval folk legend about Dr Faustus, is concentrated on the last confrontation between Faustus and Mephistopheles. The time of the pact with the Devil is over: after twenty-four years of godless life, given to Faustus by Mephistopheles, the Devil appears to claim him. In most interpretations of the Faust theme in the nineteenth and twentieth centuries the Devil is presented as evil, but also as sly and ironic, a destroyer of social and internal arrangements. In Schnittke's concept these social arrangements are set by Satan and cannot be changed: in a totalitarian regime, where moral values are deprecated, the role of absolute deity is assumed by the Devil himself. He appears in various transformations throughout the opera: as the grotesque figure of a transvestite (Mephistopheles, countertenor), as a female rock singer (Mephistophila, alto), as a narrator, as chorus, and as the postman who gives Faust the fateful letter (as also in Busoni's opera). The comprehensive power of the Devil is sublimated in the triumphant tango in the third act, in which the 'two voices' Mephisto (countertenor and alto duet) tells – not without erotic relish – about the terrible torture and death of Dr Faustus (Example 2.4). This sinister dance of death, which is embedded in the field of Soviet subculture and the 'sugary' melodies of socio-realism, reveals the sphere of the Devil.

At the other end of the scale are the eternal moral categories of Christian ethics. Choral themes, imitation polyphony and the sound of the organ are the musical equivalents of this sphere. The modern Faustus is torn between these two extremes; he has deliberately sold his soul to the Devil (the system) in full consciousness of his actions. Even the price that he has to pay – his own life and insupportable suffering – loses its value in the vacuum of the time in which he lives. The inexorable chorale in the epilogue of Schnittke's *Faust*, on a text from St Peter: 'Seid nüchtern und wachet' (Be sober and watchful), stresses the end of this 'bad and good Christian'. And delivers him from guilt.

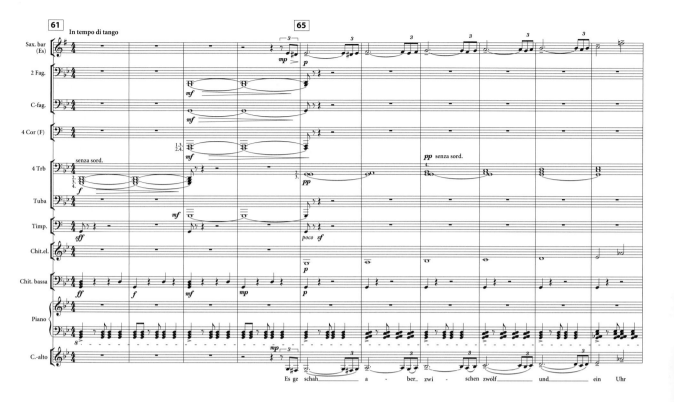

2.4 Schnittke, Faust opera, Act 3 No. 37, bars 61–70

All this is quite different in the Lenin opera *Life with an Idiot*. Beside the main characters – 'I', his wife and the mad Vova – a mad society exists, whose savage activity demolishes everything. The impersonal, anonymous power of a superior entity destroys all human individuality: not only free will and the need for freedom, but also the person himself – mentally and physically. The protagonist 'I' accepts voluntarily to take a madman from a mental institution into his own house to live with him and his wife as part of a happy family. This all would be a 'mild punishment of the collective', but also 'a hidden form of confidence', a 'mission' and even one's own personal choice. 'I' must pick out the madman according to the party's norms: the idiot must be both 'popular and national' as well as conform in 'form and content'. In contrast to the saint-like character of Yurodiviy in the Pushkin–Mussorgsky *Boris Godunov*, who represents the voice of the people and gives a prophetic meaning to the tragedy, the near human Vova, a Lenin caricature, is a grotesque Devil's deathmask in the realm of the banal. As Vova cannot articulate human speech, his vocal part is based on an inarticulate sound, and the music characterising him is 'stitched' together like a carnival costume from little pieces of Soviet popular and revolutionary songs: the Internationale, Song of the Workers, Vashavjanka, etc.

It is evident that the good–evil, devil–human dichotomy is the essence of Schnittke's modern political mythology, independent of the concrete programme or subject in each individual case. His music world sounds at times ferocious and savage, at times sublime and conciliatory. The unpredictable expressiveness of his music, the unexpected contrasts, and, most of all, the kind of aesthetic challenge created by his polystylistic method – they all inspire the enthusiasm felt by Schnittke's fans on listening to his works. For all that, Schnittke remains true to such well-known historical genres as the concerto grosso, symphony, opera or instrumental concerto, and to the late-romantic and classical modern symphonic tradition (Mahler, Shostakovich). Similar to this latter tradition also is his adherence to the motto 'to create a New World': Schnittke never abandons his idea of music as a message for the whole of the human race.

This causes a problem for many Western experts, especially in the field of the avant-garde and post-avant-garde. Helmut Lachenmann, a very important representative of this movement in Germany, wonders about the possibility, in the twenty-first century, of finding a universal common sense and common ground in modern art (music): Is it possible to play the role of messenger in a dispersed and diffuse western society, which consists of single, separate individuals? (Lachenmann 1994: 220). (I would add, a society that oscillates between a single indifferent person and an easily manipulated crowd.)

Following this train of thought, a contemporary artist has to choose between two possibilities. The first is to create accessible semantics and in this way bring art (music) closer to the people. In this case, the danger arises of degradation of the art: the art object is reduced to a consumable product. The second is based on innovation: the author searches for a new syntax, free of clichés and familiar associations. This work is intended to escape triviality, but it is only appreciated by its creator and a few selected experts; it does not reach a large audience. As a matter of fact, there are innumerable possibilities between these two extremes, in which every great artist can find a field and an audience; art without an audience is only illusion. The music of Schnittke shows that. Like his Peer Gynt, whose identity exists only because of Solveig's love, his music only exists because the audience loves it. We are confronted with a social phenomenon that needs to be explained: the oeuvre of this modern composer reaches a global culture market without being commercial.

The answer to this puzzle is to be found in the post-modern epoch itself, where such discrete elements as life and art, kitsch and consumerism, sublimity and triviality, the small elite and the masses are an indivisible entity. There is no place left for any kind of hierarchy; the surface of the artistic whole is constantly changing its position, it expands in all directions. This peculiar universal texture, which is permanently moving and whose parts cannot be recognised because of its compressed condition, corresponds to Schnittke's polystylistic method. The interplay of different historical and cultural contexts results in a multiplicity of dimensions with variable speed, intensity and expandability. This holistic form, arising from many simultaneous layers, is open, discontinued and complex. It presents a universe in which every element is correlated to everything else because of the impossibility of separating the parts from the whole, the subject from the object. The object becomes the process; the local becomes global. This is the paradigm of modern art, where there is no 'either' and 'or', but 'and' and 'also': a world where everything is possible and nothing can be anticipated. This is also the secret of Schnittke's music: it is an endless wandering between the music worlds, but it is also his own wandering between 'this' and 'another' reality, between 'here' and 'there': a psychogram of this one artist.

References

Gross, Thomas (2000) 'Satanische Verve', *Die Zeit*, 48:23 (November), pp 49–50.

Ivashkin, A. (1996) *Alfred Schnittke*, London.

Lachenmann, H. (1994) 'Freunde Alfred Schnittkes gratulieren', in *Alfred Schnittke zum 60. Geburtstag. Eine Festschrift*, Hamburg.

Schnittke, A. (1994a) 'Polistilisticeskie tendencii v sovremennoj muzyke' (Polystilistic tendencies in contemporary music), in *Besedy's A Schnittke (Dialogues with A. Schnittke)*, Moscow.

Schnittke, A. (1994b) 'Concerto Grosso Nr. 1', in *Alfred Schnittke zum 60. Geburtstag. Eine Festschrift*, Hamburg.

Schnittke, A. (1994c) 'Sinfonie Nr. 1', in *Alfred Schnittke zum 60. Geburtstag. Eine Festschrift*, Hamburg.

Alfred Schnittke
and Gustav Mahler

Georg Borchardt

Translated by
Suzan Meves

Based on a transcript of
a talk given at the
Seeking the Soul
Schnittke Festival,
Barbican Arts and
Guildhall School of
Music & Drama,
London, January 2001

Alfred Schnittke was 13 years old when he first came into contact with Gustav Mahler. At this time he was living with his parents in Vienna, and his piano teacher, Charlotte Ruber, gave him a facsimile of the score of Mahler's unfinished Tenth Symphony. She could not foresee what was to become of her pupil and the significance of her gift, but she must have been quite shrewd. The boy was especially impressed with the heartrending confessions that Mahler noted in his sketches and which were addressed to his wife Alma Mahler. 'Living for you! Dying for you! Almschi! Farewell! You alone know what it means!'. Or another desperate cry as in the scherzo: 'The devil dances it with me!' Or, elsewhere, 'Madness, touch me, the damned! Destroy me so that I forget who I am, that I stop existing … Mercy! Oh God, oh God, why have you forsaken me?' I spoke at length with Alfred Schnittke in Hamburg in 1993 on his relationship to Mahler. He told me that he had studied Mahler's score of his Tenth Symphony. When I asked him if he could imagine a connection between this music and his own, he replied:

> I thank you for this question! I love the Tenth Symphony above all, but I would perhaps not approach this task as it could be too difficult for me. I am busy with too many other ideas and should any time be left, I would certainly try it. But I certainly don't know what the result would be.

Schnittke's heart had been won by another Mahler fragment – in comparison to the torso of the Tenth merely a tiny little piece, the beginning of a movement for a Piano Quartet in G minor. This small piece is connected to the piano quartet movement in A minor that Mahler composed aged 16. The completed part of the G-minor fragment extends to the 13th bar; it then

28

becomes a sketch existing only of piano notes up to the 26th bar (Example 3.1). Peter Ruzicka published it as an addendum to the A minor Piano Quartet edited by the Sikorski Publishing House. Regarding the fragment in G minor, Schnittke said to Alexander Ivashkin: 'The theme is brilliant. This is incomparable Mahler, recognisable from the first measure. And it cannot be compared to anything else. The modulation from G minor to A major, followed by A minor – it is so unusual!' (Schnittke 1998: 242). Schnittke later went even further to say about this fragment: 'The Mahler of the Tenth Symphony seems to be shining through here' (Schnittke 1994: 122).

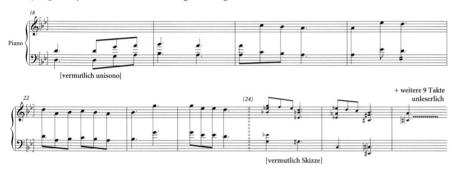

3.1 Mahler, Piano Quartet, fragment in G minor, bars 18–27

In conversation with me, Schnittke spoke of this fragment composed by the young Mahler and of which he was so fond. He said:

> Much contained therein was and remains a problem for me. I would not be able to find a single explanation, but rather two if I undertook a harmonic analysis – and it could be interpreted this way or that. I believe I have never found this ever – the lacking of finality. I remember that I thought for a long time how I could continue the composition of this work. I tried for years to find a continuation of these measures composed by Mahler. And then I imagined it not as a continuation but rather music that would approach Mahler's music – as a reminder that the end will come, and that was the solution. At first the attempt to remember and then remembrance itself.

Schnittke actually did compose a the ⊙ *piano quartet* as a paraphrase or variation on the Mahler fragment. At the place of highest sound development, he lets the piano sound stand still as a cloud of sound, and as it is fading away Mahler's music commences. However, it must be said that Schnittke only added something at the end that was not included in

⊙ The *piano quartet* is on the included CD, track 6

29

Mahler's notes. The last chord could be interpreted as an A-major chord, but possibly as F-sharp minor as well. And Schnittke imprints in the harmony of all four instruments a musical seal – a special sound. Using Peter Ruzicka's edition, in which Mahler uses A and C-sharp, Schnittke adds a C. This results in a simultaneous sound of major and minor, as can be heard in Mahler's Second and Seventh Symphonies.

But this is not all. Schnittke also added B-flat and B, and this means that we are dealing with a small cluster formed on the notes B-A-C-H (Example 3.2): in German note-letters the translation of the alphabetic letters make up Bach's name. The B-A-C-H motif is frequently found in Schnittke's compositions; he admitted that this motif has pursued him, as an obsession. With this seal, Schnittke brought Mahler's short fragment into the realm of Mahler's late Ninth and Tenth Symphonies. Schnittke's occupation with Mahler's fragment did not end with the composition of his piano quartet.

3.2 Schnittke, Piano Quartet, last movement, bars 200–5

Schnittke arranged his Mahler paraphrase for grand orchestra and made it the second movement of his Fifth Symphony. The Mahler fragment in G minor quoted at the end was retained in the piano quartet version. This is an unprecedented occurrence in the history of the symphony – a quotation, nearly in original form; a short piece of chamber music in a symphony – a unique homage to Mahler's genius. This quotation in the Fifth Symphony is the closest connection between Schnittke's and Mahler's music. The Fifth Symphony was composed as a commission for the 100th anniversary of the Concertgebouw Orchestra in Amsterdam. The orchestra was closely associated to Mahler through Willem Mengelberg, and this is also one of the reasons that Schnittke felt his commissioned work to be so closely connected to Mahler.

For Schnittke, the Fifth Symphony also was the work involving both a loving and critical analysis of Mahler – at the same time convergence and estrangement – a characteristic ambiguity for Schnittke. He wrote:

For years I considered doing something with Mahler. In my Fifth Symphony, the illusory world of the Concerto Grosso is consciously combined with false pathos and with the brutal, but in the meantime broken, world of Mahler. The third movement develops towards the sonata form – with a slow introduction and dramatic development which changes into a slow funeral reprise in the Fourth movement and a lovely madness epilogue – which then does not come into being – and it ends after a short outcry in final resignation. (Schnittke 1994: 90)

Schnittke's music is affected by the eloquence of Mahler's music. He called the dynamic climax in the final movement of his Fifth Symphony an 'outcry'. This recalls Mahler's commentary on his Second Symphony; in which he calls the outburst in the scherzo an 'outcry of desperation'.

It can be said that Schnittke's intimate relationship to the rudimentary early Mahler is the attempt of an approach to something drawn from afar – a deliberate distance in order to avoid an imaginary proximity. He distinguishes sharply between what he considers to be 'organic' and what is not. He said to me about the Mahler quotation in his piano quartet and in the Fifth Symphony: 'This connection between the quoted music and stylistically foreign matters seemed inexplicable in words to me, but it appeared to be organic'. And then he added something remarkable: 'Maybe it could be done again. And maybe it could have been pursued further'.

To pursue – getting to the music that Mahler did not compose: this does sound highly speculative. Schnittke named the logically impossible 'a reminder of something that never came into being'. He firmly believed in the idea of a pre-existential music. In a conversation with Julia Makeyeva and Gennadi Zypin, he stated:

My task is not to create music but to *hear*. The main thing is not to bother my ear when listening to something that exists outside of me. The world intoned by a composer exists outside of him, he can only attempt to seek a connection to it more or less successfully. And my work exists in my not being bothered by sham ideas formed in my head; not to banish what I hear. I strive to come as close as possible to ideal hearing, but I can never achieve total perfection in this … I repeat: It is my task not to banish what already existed on its own. I gained this realisation a long time ago. I am not the result, merely the tool. (Schnittke 1994: 22)

Schnittke's idea of producing music coincides entirely with Gustav Mahler's conviction: 'One does not compose, one is composed', wrote

Mahler in a letter. And in another letter he speaks of the 'holy conception' and describes it as 'intuition', when he suddenly finds the long-sought text for the final movement of the Second Symphony. This is what happened on the morning of 29 March 1894, during the funeral service for conductor Hans von Bülow in St Michael's Church in Hamburg, when the boys' choir intonated Friedrich Gottlieb Klopstock's chorale: 'Auferstehn, ja auferstehn wirst du mein Staub, nach kurzer Ruh' (Rise again, yea, though shalt rise again, my dust, after brief rest). Schnittke believed that as a composer he was merely a tool. Mahler said: 'One is more or less just an instrument on which the universe plays' (letter to Anna von Mildenburg, 28 June 1896).

According to Alfred Schnittke, a composer should be able to remember non-composed music. He explained this paradoxical wording as an attempt to complete Mahler's fragment: 'A recollection of something that never came into being'. The Mahler fragment Schnittke loved so dearly made a deep impression on the Russian's Seventh Symphony. It begins with a delicate allusion to Mahler's violin theme, in a major–minor variant: a solo violin cadenza is a very useful beginning for a symphony (Example 3.3).

3.3 Schnittke, Symphony No. 7, 1st mvt, bars 1–7

In the final movement of this very same symphony, No. 7, Schnittke becomes even more obvious in his reference to the Mahler theme in G minor, in an episode played by four horns. The symphony ends with a sad and macabre waltz – which actually does not come to an end, but rather remains open. These lamenting melodies are connected to Mahler's 'scherzo-like lullaby', as Schnittke described the Mahler fragment. At the end of the Seventh Symphony this melody seems to develop into a lulling sleep of death (Example 3.4).

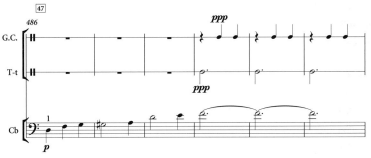

3.4 Schnittke, Symphony No. 7, last mvt, bars 486–91

32

The end of Schnittke's Seventh Symphony, with its tragicomic double bass, also reminds one of the funeral march in Mahler's First Symphony. This funeral march was a key experience for Schnittke, as the Symphony No. 1 was the first Mahler work Schnittke ever heard in a concert. He was at this time in his mid-twenties and the reason for his coming into contact with Mahler's music so late was due to the fact that performances of Mahler's symphonies in the then Soviet Union were a good deal rarer than in the West. We are all aware of the importance of the concept of polystylistics for Schnittke. In our talk he said:

> I see the beginning of polystylistics in Mahler in the First Symphony in the third movement, in the canon – it appears to me to be a concurrence of seriousness and scorn – a funeral atmosphere that several times quite unexpectedly turns into something else. This impressed me the first time I heard it, and I still have the same impression.

When Schnittke told me this, I could not know just how literally this was meant, that he still felt the impression of first hearing Mahler's funeral march. This was in June 1993 – and he was then working on his Seventh Symphony.

In a conversation with Alexander Ivashkin, Schnittke said:

> I sincerely wish to have much in common with Mahler. Yet Mahler is such a great figure for me that I would never dare to measure myself by him. Wagner is even greater than Mahler but I do not feel so close to him. A great deal separates us as well – what is present in Mahler is almost entirely missing in me. For instance, his inspired folk tunes, the *Lieder eines fahrenden Gesellen* or *Des Knaben Wunderhorn*. I could cry that I cannot compose something like this. (Schnittke 1998: 242)

Speaking to me, he voiced certain reservations in his judgement of Mahler's symphonies, despite his great admiration. In answer to my question, which Mahler symphony he liked best, Schnittke said:

> Except the First and the Tenth, I would name the Second, the Fourth, the Ninth, the Third and the Fifth – especially the Second: it is inexplicable, eternal … I cannot understand the form at all, yet I submit to this music. And the same holds true of the Ninth, which cannot be grasped intellectually, but somehow else. The Sixth and the Seventh Symphonies do not seem to me to be what those mentioned are. The

Sixth, the Seventh and the Eighth – this appears to be a path that was not followed to the end.

I asked Schnittke to explain to me what he meant by the 'path that was not followed to the end' and he answered:

> Mahler's Eighth would be the most obvious expression of an alienation that had already begun, before the Eighth Symphony – in the Seventh, or the Sixth – excuse me – even in some sections of the Fifth Symphony. It could have been an attempt to somehow become detached from oneself. And the presence of sketches for the Tenth Symphony is especially convincing. The Eighth Symphony impressed me very much, but I still have not overcome certain doubts. The Eighth is a very good work, but it did not come from within. This is inexplicable to me. The Eighth is done very well – but it is contrived. It changes into something else – something not Mahleresque.

Religiousness is an important form of contact between Gustav Mahler and Alfred Schnittke. Similar to Mahler, Schnittke was a deeply religious person. Mahler came from a Jewish family in Bohemia, but he grew up in a German-speaking world. Schnittke's father was a German Jew, his mother's ancestors came from Southern Germany – from Swabia – and had emigrated to Russia. Alfred was born in Russia and grew up bilingually. His mother tongue was that of the so-called Volga Germans – an ancient idiom that Schnittke called 'fallen asleep German'. Whoever heard him speak could believe themselves back in eighteenth-century Germany due to some of the old-fashioned expressions he used. Schnittke confessed to embracing his mother's religion and joked, 'I am half Catholic'. And yet he was not one in the sense of a dogmatically formed religion. Mahler had had very little contact with the Jewish religion in his childhood. His conversion to Catholicism has often been suspected of being opportunistic (in the sense of Heinrich Heine's *aperçu* that 'baptism is the admission ticket to European culture'). He certainly would not have become director of the Vienna Court Opera without being baptised. Actually, Mahler sympathised with Christianity quite early in his life, but his feelings were definitely interdenominational.

Schnittke and Mahler both have the use of the crucifix in their music in common. Schnittke went even further and declared: 'I would compare what happens in composition to a crucifix where the framework of the cross and the flesh nailed onto it must become apparent.' Gottfried Eberle proved the structure of the crucifix in Schnittke's Piano Quintet (Eberle 1994: 46–54).

In Mahler's First and Second Symphonies, the cross appears as an intonation made up of three tones: G-A-C. His three-tone formula dates back to the Medieval Gregorian chant and is used in different connections to denote the crucifix. Franz Liszt knew and used this formula explicitly as 'a tonic symbol of the cross'. Richard Wagner takes it up in *Parsifal* as the motif of the Grail – in combination with the so-called 'Dresden Amen'. Just when Parsifal conquers his adversary Klingsor, he strikes the sign of the cross with his spear as the cross symbol is heard in the orchestra. Mahler quotes the cross symbol in the final movement of his First Symphony, and in the first movement of the Second Symphony in analogy to *Parsifal*.

It is not widely known that Alfred Schnittke's Second Violin Concerto follows a hidden programme in dramatic fashion. He obviously first planned this work to include a chorus, which was to be sung in vocalises (without text). I owe this information to the violinist Mark Lubotsky, to whom the work was dedicated, and who had been friends with Schnittke since their student days in Moscow. The concerto deals with the Passion of Jesus Christ, and with the known Stations of the Cross, beginning with the Garden of Gethsemane on Mount Olive, arrest, condemnation, torture, death on the cross and ending with the resurrection. The violin solo plays the part of Jesus and the double bass solo the figure of Judas. It appears as if Schnittke gained the inspiration for his programmatic concept from several of the 'Poems of Zhivago' contained in the epilogue of Boris Pasternak's novel *Dr Zhivago*. The poems 'Hamlet' and 'Gethsemane' are the first and last poems of this epilogue. Both poems contain the prayer: 'Father, if it is possible, then let this cup pass me by'.

Allusions to the passion of Christ can be found in two of Mahler's *Wunderhorn* Lieder. A song for soprano to the text 'Das himmlische Leben' ('Heavenly life') became the final movement of the Fourth Symphony, and the song for solo alto, boys' choir and women's choir 'Es sungen drei Engel einen süßen Gesang' ('Three Angels sang a sweet song') was later used for the fifth movement of the Third Symphony. In the final movement of the Fourth, the second verse begins thus: 'Johannes das Lämmlein auslasset, der Metzger Herodes drauf passet. Wir führen ein geduldig's, unschuldig's, ein liebliches Lämmlein zu Tod') (St John gives up his little lamb, the butcher Herod seizes it! We lead an innocent, patient lovely little lamb to death').

The text in Mahler's Third Symphony relates to an episode preceding the account of the Passion. 'And as the Lord Jesus sat at the table, eating supper with his twelve disciples, the Lord Jesus spoke: "Why are you standing here? When I look at you, you weep!"' The person spoken to is Peter and he answers: 'And I should not weep, you gracious God, I have broken the Ten Commandments. I go and weep bitterly' (the angels interrupt him here with an additional text by Mahler: 'You should not weep'), 'ah come and have mercy on me'. It is revealing that the orchestration Mahler uses here is very similar to the music of the Lamb of God led to death in the song for soprano. He relates Peter's weeping to the episode in Pilate's palace, where the apostle denies knowing Jesus. A reported conversation of Mahler's in early July 1896, when he was working on his Third Symphony, is interesting in this respect. He was speaking to his friend, violinist Natalie Bauer-Lechner. She wrote down all her conversations with Mahler and obviously took great pains in recounting the words of the composer she regarded so highly. They are undoubtedly authentic. Mahler went out walking with her after a busy morning's work and said:

> I am truly horrified to see where this leads to, what path it is forced to take and that I have been given the terrible task of being the carrier of this gigantic work. Today I felt as when something experienced suddenly lights up and becomes apparent as something already known: Christ on Mount Olive, who must empty the cup of suffering to the last drop and – desired this. For whom this cup is meant, cannot and does not want to refuse it, yet at the same time a deathly fear must come over him, when he thinks of what still lies ahead.

Mahler identifies himself with the martyr and this also holds true of Alfred Schnittke, who through Pasternak's tragic fate had a foreboding of what could happen to him in Soviet Russia.

Alfred Schnittke and Mahler are related in spirit by the fact that, as symphonic composers, they both include the religious sphere in their music – Mahler in his Second, Third and Eighth Symphonies, Schnittke in his Second and Fourth Symphonies. I also see an analogy between the two composers in the use of the word 'shadow'. Mahler's scores use the term *schattenhaft* ('shadowy') on several occasions, such as in the Seventh, Ninth and Tenth Symphonies. When I asked Alfred Schnittke if his term *Schattenwelt* ('shadow world') could possibly coincide with Mahler's term *schattenhaft*, he answered evasively. I reminded him of his conversation with Julia Makayeva and Gennadi Zypin in 1988, and I would like to quote the following remarks Schnittke made:

> In my mind, this is a world of illusion, unlimited and endless. It has a sphere of shadow – which is not written down in notes, and which leaves no traces. And there is an area no longer that of the shadow, but of actual being – that which has remained. In this sense that which

Mozart succeeded in composing exists in the real sphere, and in the shadowy, unreal sphere is the enormous world of sound that he did not succeed in creating. It can even be presumed that this unrealised Mozart is endless, as Bach and all the other great composers are endless. Real music is only a small part of an immeasurable world with which man has to deal. And if he is attentive, he will feel it, this enormous, illusionary musical world. (Schnittke 1994: 22)

I am convinced that Schnittke comes very close here to Mahler's world of thought. During the course of our conversation, Alfred Schnittke and I discussed Mahler's brokenness and he said: 'I think Mahler had brokenness – consciously or not – and it existed in him – as well as in the structure of his symphonies. This appears to be an eternal law of life and development'. What Schnittke formulated here could also be said about himself and his work. He suffered painful breaks during the course of his life and he was called back from the brink of death several times. Hard to define, minute cracks and crevices also intersperse Schnittke's music, which appears to reflect an intact world. Mahler's late works – the Tenth Symphony, above all, the final movements of the *Lied von der Erde* and the Ninth Symphony – influenced many a work from the last decade of Schnittke's life, especially the Eighth Symphony. A feeling for time leading to eternity – such as in the final movement of the *Lied von der Erde* and in the epilogue of *Peer Gynt* – belong to the two composers' spiritual affinity. In his *Cantata on Poems of the Fifteenth and Sixteenth Centuries*, Schnittke set to music a text by the German mystic Jakob Böhme, which would probably have delighted Mahler. 'To whom time is as eternity and eternity as time, he is freed of all strife'. In the draft of his Ninth Symphony, Mahler noted a title on the sketch of his scherzo: 'Menuetto infinito'. And finally Mahler and Schnittke shared a feeling for reckless humour and for the permanent, absurd tragicomedy of life.

References

Eberle, Gottfried (1994) 'Figur und Struktur von Kreuz und Kreis am Beispiel von Alfred Schnittkes Klavierquintett', in *Alfred Schnittke zum 60. Geburtstag. Eine Festschrift*, Hamburg.

Schnittke, Alfred (1994) *Alfred Schnittke zum 60. Geburtstag. Eine Festschrift*, Hamburg.

Schnittke, Alfred (1998) *Über das Leben und die Musik–Gespräche mit Alexander Iwaschkin*, München and Düsseldorf.

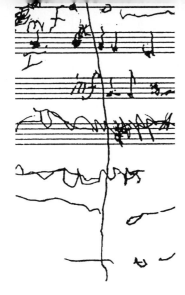

Alfred Schnittke's works:
a new theory of musical content

Valentina Kholopova

Based on a transcript of
a talk given at the
Seeking the Soul
Schnittke Festival,
Barbican Arts and
Guildhall School of
Music & Drama,
London, January 2001

Traditionally, the theory of music implies various fields of knowledge concerning compositional techniques, including harmony, polyphony, musical form, and instrumentation. However, for many modern musical compositions these techniques are not enough to give us the insight we need. Nor can a general aesthetic theory help us, because it is not specific enough about music. To complement this technical theory of music, we need to turn to a theory of musical content. Such a theory could be seen to consist of three integral parts:

1. The portrayal of emotions through music.
2. Musical description, or 'painting'.
3. Musical symbolism.

It is the first of these aspects, the portrayal of emotion, – is vital the other two aspects may or may not be utilised.

Turning to music composed at the end of the twentieth and beginning of the twenty-first centuries, we can find examples of each of these three aspects. The expression of extreme emotions can be found, and whereas musical 'painting' is comparatively unpopular, the use of musical symbolism is much more widespread and takes on an increasingly important role.

All of these three aspects can thus be found in Alfred Schnittke's music, and it is interesting to investigate the personal way the Russian composer makes use of them. He is interested in strong emotional expression: intense expressiveness distinguishes the climaxes in all his symphonies, and peaks of intensity characterise his operatic vocal writing (as in *Gesualdo*). Dry pointillism, on the other hand, never attracted him, and he employed this style exclusively as an ironical device, as in the Concert Grosso No. 1.

Musical 'painting' did not much interest Schnittke, either, although it is possible to find instances of this type of musical description, such as the orchestral descriptions of the words 'night was coming' and 'revealed the mystery to him' in his *Faust* cantata. In addition, Schnittke utilised a number of devices from early musical rhetoric (widely used by composers in the sixteenth, seventeenth and eighteenth centuries) - in his *Faust* cantata, for example, the words 'infamous pride' are sung in ascending motion (the figure of *anabasis*), and the words about the sand-glass, 'the sand is running out', in descending step-wise motion (the figure of *catabasis*).

However, musical symbolism was important to the composer: his music is rich in all kinds of musical symbols, such as the enormous number of encoded names to be found in his pieces. For example, in the Third Symphony (dedicated to the Gewandhaus Concert Hall in Leipzig) musical monogrammes (where musical themes are constructed from letter names for musical notes) represent the first and last names of thirty-three German and Austrian composers, as well as the words Gewandhaus, Leipzig, Erde, Thomaskirche, and das Bose, which help to carry the message of the piece. One of Schnittke's chamber pieces, for cello solo, is even entitled 'Sounding Letters': it is dedicated to Alexander Ivashkin and based on the letters of his name that are also found in Alfred Schnittke's name (AEADE-ASCH).

Another type of musical symbolism is the composer's assimilation of various other styles into his or her own style, while still maintaining a personal voice: Schnittke coined the term 'polystylistics' to cover this technique. In this way, Schnittke's music can reflect Baroque stylistic approaches, without his writing becoming a pastiche of Bach or Vivaldi, for example. Collage is a well-known polystylistic device.

Thus, allusions to other musics within a polystylistic approach can bring additional meanings into a composition, without having to resort to extra-musical devices such as the use of words, and those meanings can vary from one piece to another. For example, in his Third Symphony Schnittke presents the history of Austro-German music in the form of stylistic allusions, from early polyphony through the styles of Haydn, Mozart, Beethoven, Schumann, Weber, Wagner, the Second Viennese School, and many other composers, including Mauricio Kagel.

In addition, Schnittke's pieces sometimes utilise musical symbols that imply verbal texts which are not written out in the music but are recalled by the listener. For example, the 'Dies Irae' theme is used in the finale of the First Symphony, and in the First Violin Sonata for violin and piano there is a section where the dodecaphonic theme is reminiscent of the Russian folk song 'Barynia'.

Schnittke did not remain unaffected by the symbolism of numbers. One example is his 'Lebenslauf' for percussion ensemble. Written for the composer's 48th birthday, it utilises all the factors of the number 48: namely 1, 2, 3, 4, 6, 8, 12, 24 and 48.

The composer also used the symbolism of gestures and other movements made by performing musicians. The piece that is richest in gestures is the 'Three Scenes' for soprano and ensemble. The singer sings a sad melody while turning the handle of a coffee-grinder – fatally, hopelessly. Meanwhile, the percussionists (vibraphone, bass drum, cymbals) accompany their strokes by various movements of their bodies. Another kind of gesture can be seen in the Fourth Violin Concerto. In movements two and four there are climaxes where the violinist, drowned by the orchestra, pretends that he or she is playing while in fact no sounds are being produced. Schnittke writes in the score: 'cadenza visuale'. Elements of instrumental theatre are introduced into the First Symphony where, in the very opening, the musicians run onto the stage, warming up as they do so, and in the end of the second movement the entire wind section goes away into the wings to return before the finale and to play a tragicomic conglomerate of funeral marches.

Among the symbols employed by Schnittke there are also hidden programmes: for example, Judas's treachery is represented in the Second Violin Concerto. To help him portray these programmes, Schnittke used a number of rhetorical devices, and the descriptive or 'painting' techniques described above.

If we turn to one particular Schnittke work, we can see how these aspects described above have been integrated into the composition. The Sonata No. 2 for Violin and Piano, Quasi una sonata, was written in 1968 and is dedicated to its first performers: Mark Lubotsky and Ljuba Yedlina.

The emotional content of the Second Violin Sonata is unusually intense: Schnittke told me that here he wanted an unlimited musical expressiveness, that both violinist and pianist are to strain to the limit of their musical and physical capacities. To help unleash the performers' expression, the violin part employs all the novel techniques of the time: free playing around the written notes without a specific metre, chords in the highest register, pizzicato and glissando, pointillistic 'ragged' texture, and so on. The piano employs simultaneous clusters, tremolo clusters, 'moving' clusters (up and down, forth and back). These expressive moments come to a climax at the Allegretto section: a frantic repetition of the fortissimo G-minor chord 114 times, alternating with other chords (see Example 4.1).

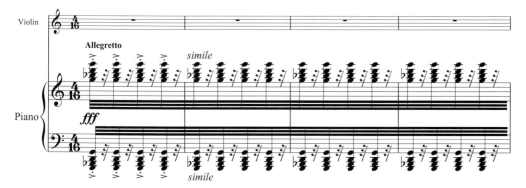

4.1 Schnittke, Violin Sonata No. 2, bars 322-5

Certain musical movements are extremely strong and acute. For example, the first chord sounds like a shot, loud and sharp. This is followed by a shrill, dissonant chord on the violin, like a howl. The last violin chord, meant to provide reconciliation, is also dissonant: it is the G-minor triad with a split third (b flat and b natural).

The emotional contrasts within the composition are extremely intense. Here Schnittke embodies the idea of a contrast between the disharmony of the contemporary world and the harmony of the past. That is why, by contrast with emotions of aggressiveness and frantic tension, he also introduces into the sonata emotions of Classical elevation and even of Romantic sweetness (in the spirit of César Franck or Franz Liszt). The emotional world of the Second Sonata is not only extremely intense but also vast and varied.

We do not find examples of the descriptive or 'painting' musical techniques in the Sonata, but on the other hand musical symbolism is much in evidence and it can be found at a number of different levels. Let us begin with the title 'Quasi una sonata'. This is a symbolic allusion to the subtitle of Beethoven's Piano Sonatas Nos. 13 and 14 'Quasi una fantasia'. By 'quasi sonata' Schnittke means a parody of a sonata, in which its traditional form is distorted; all the movements and the subjects are logically displaced. The opening, which states the main idea, is not the first subject but only an introduction, while the tremolo clusters in the piano part (see example 4.2), which seem to serve as a background, are in the composer's mind the first subject of the piano part. The tremolo performed with the wood of the bow, in the violin part (see example 4.3) is in fact the first subject of that instrument's part. The second subject is not easy to find either: it begins from the Moderato (see example 4.4). The frantic climax of the whole sonata (with the 114 G-minor chords; example ?.1, above), comprising the centre of development, is the coda.

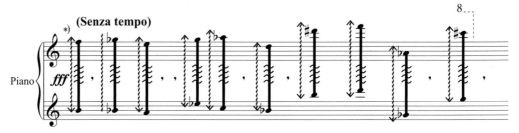

*Tremoli in irregular sequence within the range of the cluster

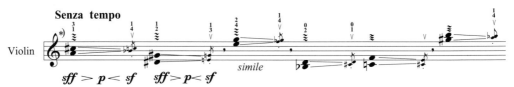

*Tremoli in irregular sequence col legno with ricochet with short lingering on the second interval

4.4 Schnittke, Violin Sonata No. 2, bars 79–82

Schnittke also told me that in the opening of the Sonata he saw the violinist and pianist as the still figures of Solomon Mihoels' theatre (Mihoels was a famous Soviet theatre director murdered on Stalin's orders): hence the manner in which the sonata should be played. After the first chord, the pianist should stay still with his or her hands tense over the keyboard for six seconds. The violinist, after the sharply dissonant opening chord, is to hold the bow in the air for ten seconds, without putting it down.

The sonata contains the letter-symbol BACH, the symbol of the beauty and magnificence of old music (see Example 4.5). It also has a symbol in the form of a quotation from the middle of the so-called 'Prometheus' theme from Beethoven's 33 Variations for Piano (see Example 4.6).

In addition, there are symbols in the sonata of the type that Schnittke called 'quotations of styles' or 'polystylistics': these are not actual quotations, but themes in the style of Liszt and Brahms. (See the quotations of Liszt's style together with the BACH motif in example 4.5, above. For the quotation of Brahms' style together with the BACH motif see example 4.7.)

4.5 Schnittke, Violin Sonata No. 2, bars 196–201

4.6 Schnittke, Violin Sonata No. 2, bars 249–52

4.7 Schnittke, Violin Sonata No. 2, bar s 257–8

This is the music of Romantic sweetness mentioned above.

Thus, I have named five kinds of musical symbolism in Schnittke's sonata:

1. A play on genres – 'Quasi una sonata'.
2. The theatrical allusion in the motionless figures of the instrumentalists.
3. The letter-symbols spelling BACH.
4. The quotation from Beethoven's 33 Variations for Piano.
5. The polystylistic assimilation of the musical styles of Liszt and Brahms.

Is it possible to give a faithful performance of this sonata without knowledge of the symbolism contained within it? I think not: if one wants to embody the idea of Schnittke all of this needs to be understood. The most memorable performances of the sonata that I have heard were prepared with the help of the composer's own commentary.

Nineteenth-century music – Schumann, Tchaikovsky, Verdi – can be passed, as they used to say in those times, 'from heart to heart'. But for twentieth-century music we cannot rely solely on our emotions – we must use also our reason and our intellect.

Alfred Schnittke, at home in Moscow, 1978

*Alfred and
Irina Schnittke,
in Stockholm for
the Alfred Schnittke
Festival, 1989*

Schnittke's Violin Sonata No. 2 as an open commentary on the composition of modern music

Paul Westwood

Paper presented at Guildhall School of Music & Drama during the Seeking the Soul Schnittke Festival, London, January 2001

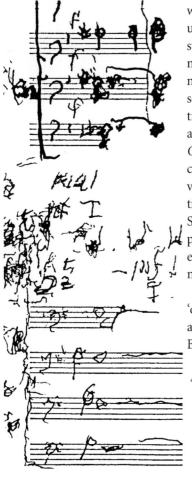

Alfred Schnittke's Violin Sonata No. 2 (1968) depicts a free atonal music being intruded by elements from tonal composition. In its argument, Schnittke distorts ideas from the sonata tradition and questions their truth in an era where the nature of compositional form has dramatically changed. This runs in consequence with his own development as a composer and his experiences working with tonal and atonal materials. Schnittke's music of the late 1960s signalled a departure from his working with dodecaphony in the earlier part of the decade to creating freer structures using a more experimental approach. Schnittke's abandonment of existing systems allowed his works greater intention in both their musical and extra-musical ideas. His Serenade (1968) piled up musical quotations from light music and Russian masterpieces, creating a town band parody that consciously attempted to integrate popular and classical music. An entirely contrasting work, Pianissimo (1968) for orchestra, built up small resonances to a huge mass, being based on ideas from Franz Kakfa's short story *In The Penal Colony*. With such release from the constraints of strict compositional principles, it is curious to see in Schnittke's catalogue of works from this period a violin sonata: one of classical music's most conservative forms of composition, for a traditional pairing of violin and piano. This sonata, the Violin Sonata No. 2 (1968), extends beyond its title to become a commentary on the position of the sonata in modern music. It is a problematic work in its inherent objective to comment on the position of the sonata in twentieth-century music, because it also has to pass judgement on itself.

The problem is further exacerbated by the work's self-doubting subtitle 'quasi una sonata', which conveys a serious ambiguity yet at the same time a humorous apology, but this elusive phrase can be traced to other sources. Beethoven used 'quasi una fantasia' as a subheading on a piano sonata (No.

46

13 in E flat), and *Quasi una fantasia* is also the title of a compilation of writings on modern music by Theodor Adorno, published in 1963. It is a possibility that Schnittke may have borrowed and altered the subtitle of his sonata from one of these sources, as the Adorno book contains a few glimpses of ideas which surface in the Schnittke sonata. In an essay titled 'Berg's Discoveries in Compositional Technique', Adorno writes:

> Composers now work in terms of 'areas', instead of themes and thematic complexes. A path leads from each area to the next, but none is the logical inference or result of its predecessor. They all have equal status and stand on the same plane. They serve as the prototypes of what must become of the symphonic form once the sonata system, and even more importantly, the spirit of the sonata, has been exhausted. (Adorno 1992: 190)

Schnittke's compositional style in the Violin Sonata No. 2 resembles in some aspects what Adorno prescribes for the future of the 'sonata'. The sonata is heavily fragmented, with many sections bearing little resemblance to what has come before or what is to follow, although the linkage between sections means that there is no sense of disjointment. However, Schnittke at the same time holds the sonata together with returning developments, in particular a strong G-minor chord in the piano which often creates disturbances throughout the piece, and he uses the archaic B-A-C-H motif as the pitch material for several sections. Therefore, many aspects of the work's material place it outside of Adorno's prescription, but Schnittke in this sonata communicates a similar message to Adorno, that of the handling of the musical form when working with atonal materials. The fragmentation of Schnittke's Violin Sonata No. 2, especially in the opening where tiny cells of material are announced amongst long silences, gives the impression that 'the spirit of the sonata has been exhausted' in quite a literal sense. If Schnittke had reference to Adorno's *Quasi una fantasia* at the time of writing the sonata, which he may have done since by accounts he had a comprehensive library of modern music materials (Ivashkin 1996: 86), then the ideas in the book may well have been an inspiration to him.

The Schnittke work reflects on elements of the sonata, such as the cadenza and the ordering of materials, attempting to find new ways for these to exist within the style of composition. The survival of the 'sonata' through changes in musical language is due to its ethos being central to the compositional process, that of statement and development. The abandonment of tonal centre characterising much music from the twentieth century poses a problem for the sonata, which traditionally operated on a resolved argument between tonally different subject groups finally balanced by an affirmation of the home key. Serial music, such as that practised by Boulez and Stockhausen in the 1950s, and the chance music of John Cage both created their own structural agendas, based in the former on the potential of row material, and in the latter by coin tosses. Pierre Boulez's famous Third Piano Sonata (1957–8) demonstrated the potential of the sonata as an open form, devising a mobile system whereby the pianist can perform the work via a number of routes. His article concerning this piece, *Sonate, que me veux-tu?* (1960), is not favourable to total indeterminacy, instead commending the merits of a composer's decisions in regard to his material and intentions (Jameux 1991: 95). The development of his material, referencing medieval forms such as trope and *cantus firmus*, contrasted with the changeable order of sections, consciously breaks the chronological sonata model, with the musical argument being subject to a variety of progressions. In the Schnittke sonata, there are sections that re-emerge in altered form throughout the work, appearing each time with insistence as if their statement had been previously incomplete. There is much recapitulation of material in the Schnittke, which often, instead of being an outcome of an argument, will interpolate a section already underway, also suggesting a reordering of the expected sonata process. The sudden rearrival of material, and the fast succession of sections in the work, has affinities with techniques used in film and cartoon music; writing music to accompany visuals was Schnittke's main occupation as a Mosfilm composer. The sonata emerged in the same year he was working on Andrey Khrzhanovsky's cartoon *Glass Accordion*, which featured collages of established works of art (Ivashkin 1996: 110–11). Schnittke's contribution to the cartoon was a score which gathered together many different types of music, in a similar manner to the rapid exchange of styles in his sonata, although this sonata is focused more on 'modern' musical styles.

The frequent changing of style in the Violin Sonata No. 2 requires a versatile notation as a stimulus for the performer. Despite its fragmentary nature, the sonata does not incorporate possibilities for the performers to reorder the material, otherwise this would destroy the chronology of the work's gradually increasing tension. Indeterminacy does play a role in some areas of the music, especially for one passage marked 'senza tempo', where most of the note-beaming has disappeared and the performers are instructed to play the material according to its appearance on the page. The violin is given a long and painstakingly detailed glissando to play here, which the performer is to approximate and temporally adjust alongside the piano's material (Example 5.1).

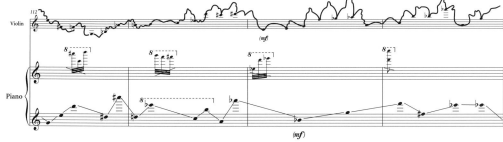

5.1 Schnittke, Violin Sonata No. 2, bars 112–15

The notation of the glissando like a geographical figure sprawling across the stave, sometimes going backwards on itself, is very much like the detailed glissando notation of John Cage's Concert For Piano And Orchestra (1958), as are the approximate relation between parts (Example 5.2).

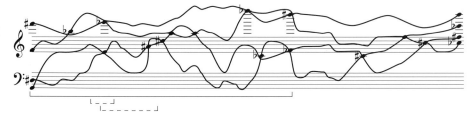

5.2 Cage, Concert for Piano and Orchestra, piano part, section M

Schnittke also employs many notations found in twentieth-century works designating types of clusters and harmonics, and for the violin quarter-tones, displaying his recognition and subsequent incorporation of twentieth-century ideas and techniques.

Another essay in Adorno's *Quasi una fantasia*, with the title 'Vers une musique informelle' hypothesises an 'informal music', which the writer describes as being 'a type of music which has discarded all forms which are external or abstract or which confront it in an inflexible way' (Adorno 1992: 272), in other words a music which is not governed by formal procedures. Although Schnittke's sonata makes several references to external forms in its argument, there are many sections of the work, particularly early on, where the choice of notes and their progression do not follow a particular schematic logic and instead seem to have been chosen by the composer in order to create a free commentary, rather than to determine a closed structure. In other sections of the work, however, the musical material is contained within an explicit structure, such as a chorale or fugue, where Schnittke wittily sets the B-A-C-H motif within a baroque model. As a whole, the sonata does not adhere to Adorno's principle, due to its conscious tonal–atonal dichotomy, but certainly pays homage to the idea of free composition in some of its passages. Schnittke's music, however, could be termed 'free' in the sense that the composer is able to complement and work with a variety of external musical forms, rather than compromising with a particular school of composition. Adorno believes that music must pursue its objective without the control of external forms, whereas Schnittke perceives musical freedom in absorption of styles, allowing himself the flexibility of switching between stylistic voices in order to achieve his compositional aims.

Schnittke's Violin Sonata No. 2 opens with two chords: the first is a G-minor chord on the piano, the second a discordant pile of sevenths on the violin (Example 5.3).

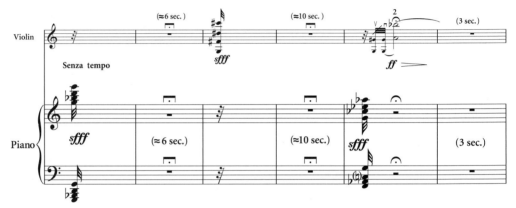

5.3 Schnittke, Violin Sonata No. 2, bars 1–6

Essentially, these two momentary statements represent the fundamental argument of this sonata. The separation of the chords by a period of silence clearly establishes these two ideas – the first an establishment of tonality, the second a rejection of it – as the two poles in the work. The opening G-minor chord reappears frequently in the piece, at each time conflicting with and preventing progression of the music, trying to forcibly establish a tonal root (Example 5.4). At the end of the sonata, the piano's G-minor chord constantly reiterates itself, attempting to drive away the violin's insistent semitones, but at the head of the conflict, the piano collapses into a cluster, leaving the violin alone to organise the ending, comprising mainly of previous statements (Example 5.5). The violin's last notes are a spread G-minor arpeggio, but arriving on a B-flat/B-natural dyad, with the discordant B natural being strongly emphasised with extra vibrato. The reluctance to resolve into a set 'home key', when considered alongside the con-

5.4 Schnittke, Violin Sonata No. 2, bars 312–13

5.5 Schnittke, Violin Sonata No. 2, bars 369–71

flict between tonal and atonal material in the work, is a truthful outcome to the argument of the music, which started with a momentarily strong tonal agenda.

Throughout the Violin Sonata No. 2, Schnittke employs one of classical music's most infamous mottos, the pitch motif bearing Bach's name. The actual notes B-A-C-H occupy a small compass in the octave, and this makes the motif ideal for atonal material, due to its ability to provide intervals such as the semitone, major seventh and minor ninth. Such intervals permeate the work excessively, resulting in a very noticeable tonal detachment and a strident modernist sound. The importance of the semitone in this sonata is pointed out after the opening where the violin, playing alone, repeats a semitone interval fourteen times with great force. This feature also occurs at the climax of the work, where the piano attempts to establish a tonal hold by repetition of an unchanging G-minor chord. The B-A-C-H motif is not deliberately announced until several minutes into the sonata, where it is the top voice in an ironically chorale-like figure, although this chorale is in a much lower registration than a Bach chorale, and is distorted by a tonally wayward bass part (Example 5.6). The motif is later used as a subject in a

5.6 Schnittke, Violin Sonata No. 2, bars 195–200

rhythmically propulsive fugue, where it is interwoven within other subjects, eventually becoming the sole theme in a busy stretto (Example 5.7).

5.7 Schnittke, Violin Sonata No. 2, bars 222–4

From here until the climax of the sonata, the motif is increasingly used as the pitches in held chords, and as a forceful figure where the diatonic 'A-C-H' notes are simultaneously contradicted by the 'B', creating the tonal conflict which is a subject of the piece (Example 5.8). The last four chords of the work, played on the violin, place the B-A-C-H motif against its retrograde, creating the final ambiguity (Example 5.9).

5.8 Schnittke, Violin Sonata No. 2, bars 263–5

5.9 Schnittke, Violin Sonata No. 2, bars 386–7

The B-A-C-H subject functions initially as an outside voice in the sonata, gradually becoming very integrated in the work, perhaps as a comment on the act of contemporary composition, where the composer's breaking off from the tradition is never an entire fulfilment. It is perhaps no coincidence that the B-A-C-H motif also plays a fundamental part in the *Glass Accordion* cartoon previously mentioned, where different musical styles are related by employment of the B-A-C-H material, again suggesting the motif to be a representation of Western art music (Ivashkin 1996: 111).

Another important element of the classical music tradition that is explored in Schnittke's Violin Sonata No. 2 is the cadenza. The work contains several passages that are marked, in a similarity to the work's subtitle, 'quasi cadenza' or 'senza tempo'. These often announce or recapitulate ideas in isolation, or in some cases explore and develop a particular instrumental effect, such as piano clusters or *tremoli col legno* on the violin. In these passages, Schnittke prepares for later development of these ideas, and also creates a necessary tension or resolution to progress into the next passage. The employment of silence in these passages not only creates a sense of expectation, but also remarks on its widespread function as a musical element in the twentieth century. Later in the work, these 'quasi cadenza' passages have become very animated exchanges between the violin and piano with small statements being responded to in a rapid argumentative manner, but always suddenly broken up by an element of a classical cadenza, the diminished seventh chord (Example 5.10). By the end of the sonata, the two instrumentalists in the 'quasi cadenza' passages are simultaneously stating material, with the piano's G-minor interjections becoming both a solution and a catalyst for the argument (Example 5.11).

It is these 'quasi cadenza' passages which provide the momentum for the work as a whole, with a perceived accelerando from the heavily sparse opening to a chaotic exchange near the end. It is interesting that the main sense of progression in this piece comes from the sections which are prescribed as tempo-less or 'free', which has possibly resulted from a conscious removal of the pulse which holds together tonal statements. The uninhibited manner in which these statements are allowed to speak allows a clear and forward-driven argument to function. However, at one point in the

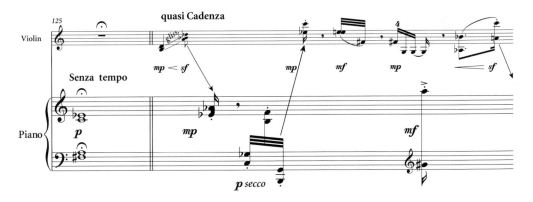

5.10 Schnittke, Violin Sonata No. 2, bars 125–6

5.11 Schnittke, Violin Sonata No. 2, bars 314–15

work, Schnittke writes a bold passage for the solo piano with the unequivocal title 'cadenza'. Here, Schnittke's intention and wit are both strong as the piano performs an extravagant series of clusters, notated pictorially, moving up and down the piano in a deliberate mockery of the intense arpeggiaic movement at the end of a classical piano cadenza. The traditional role of the cadenza, to reveal the mastery of the performer and at the same time create an opportunity for a return to the tonic key, is made to look ridiculous and unnecessary in this style of composition (Example 5.12).

The sections of this sonata which are given a pulse and a tempo direction are often fast with strict rhythm being a main element and no rubato effects, a prime example being the fugue already mentioned. The first section with an unequivocal tempo marking, Allegretto, is a mechanical exploration of the semitone and its related intervals, with a harmonically static piano part. The effect of progression largely through rhythmic momentum, instead of harmony, shares features with Cage's prepared piano music. Pulse becomes more of an important feature towards the end of the work, as its alternation with free sections creates greater tension, especially in its heavily dissonant material. There is a sense that this material does not

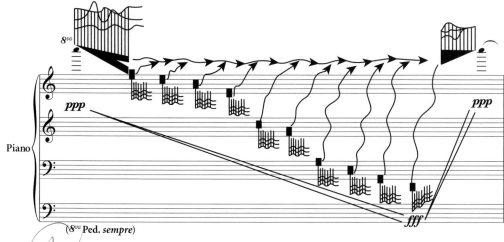

5.1/1 Schnittke, Violin Sonata No. 2, bars 314–15

belong within the strict parameters of tempo, since it is allowed to develop more openly in the tempo-less sections, again expressing the desire for atonal music to distance itself from the systems associated with tonality. Schnittke, however, does use this concept to create parody in the sonata, in a solo violin waltz after the piano cadenza, and in a march episode that suddenly cuts in after a long silence near the end of the work. In these cases he uses atonal material in order to create a disturbance in an established form, using light music to provide a sinister effect.

The ultimate question regarding Schnittke's Violin Sonata No. 2 is whether it is able to pass its own claim to being a sonata or otherwise. In comparison with the Beethoven sonata that claims itself to be 'quasi una fantasia', the Schnittke sonata, because of its free development of ideas, could be termed a fantasia which is 'quasi una sonata'. The strong element of opposition in the Schnittke work is perhaps its strongest claim to existing as a sonata, but it simultaneously comments on the relevance of its own form through rapid adoption of various styles, which destroys the balance and seamless commentary that characterises the traditional work. In calling this piece a sonata, Schnittke has exercised a right to regard it as part of a genre, but he is also conditioning the listener to expect something different to what the music actually is. Applying a plain title to the work may have also been an attempt to make it seem inconspicuous to the Soviet bureaucracy. In light of the variety of forms that have existed under the title 'symphony', the next major form Schnittke was to tackle, perhaps it was not an inappropriate decision to make. Although the model of the sonata has changed in complement of compositional trends, it appears that its titling for a work which calls for the development of contrasting ideas, even when the subject material is broad and self-referential, is still appropriate.

55

References

Adorno, Theodor (1992) *Quasi una fantasia* (trans. Rodney Livingstone), London: Verso.

Ivashkin, Alexander (1996) *Alfred Schnittke*, London: Phaidon.

Jameux, Dominique (1991) *Pierre Boulez* (trans. Susan Bradshaw), London: Faber and Faber, 1991.

LeBrecht, Norman (1992) *The Guide to 20th Century Music*, London: Simon & Schuster.

Pritchett, James (1993) *The Music of John Cage*, Cambridge: Cambridge University Press.

Schnittke, Alfred (1972) *Violin Sonata No. 2 (Quasi una sonata)*, Vienna: Universal Edition.

The interpretation of Schnittke's piano pieces: raising some questions

Maria Krivenski

W

hen I first started learning some of Schnittke's wonderful piano pieces I was eager to find out as much information as possible about their composer and the pieces themselves. I came across some very interesting material, but many of my questions about performance practice issues remained unanswered. While these questions are commonly addressed when dealing with mainstream piano repertoire no one has yet considered them in relation to this contemporary composer, Alfred Schnittke.

In this chapter a number of factors will be discussed with regard to what material is readily available to today's performer of Schnittke's piano pieces. Firstly, the 'musical' evidence – the scores themselves and the recordings that have been made of the pieces by pianists Schnittke worked with – will be considered, and then the 'extra-musical' material, which deals with information about Schnittke's relationship with the piano and with his performers.

The discussion will then focus on to the extent that these three different sources – the scores, the recordings and the extra-musical data – give us information which is useful to the performer, and where this information could be supplemented by further research.

Finally, two possible areas of research which have not, so far, been considered will be proposed, along with some examples to justify the validity and importance of research that explores them. This is accompanied by suggestions as to the sort of information that could be made available to performers to help them make intelligent and inspiring interpretative choices.

With one exception, Schnittke's piano pieces can be divided into two main sections: those written in the first half of the 1960s, and those written in the last decade of his life. To the first group belong three works: Prelude

Paper presented at Guildhall School of Music & Drama during the Seeking the Soul Schnittke Festival, London, January 2001

57

and Fugue (1963), and Improvisation and Fugue and Variations on a Chord (both 1965). In the second group we have four pieces: three sonatas (1987, 1991 and 1992) and the Five Aphorisms, a collection of short preludes written in 1990. The pieces in these two groups are all available in print. Finally, the exception is the collection Six Pieces that Schnittke wrote in 1971. To me, these pieces are a case apart, as they are, as far as I am aware, the only available example of children's pieces that Schnittke ever wrote for a solo instrument. Only four pieces of this collection are currently available in a printed edition.

Surprisingly, only one of Schnittke's dedicatees has recorded any of his solo pieces: I am referring to his wife, Irina Schnittke, who has given us a premier recording of the Second Piano Sonata. All of the published pieces have been recorded by Boris Berman, who first started collaborating with Schnittke in the mid-1960s (see Discography). As far as I am aware, none of the other pianists Schnittke collaborated with has recorded any of the piano solo pieces.

The third type of source is the extra-musical material. Although quite a lot of material has been published about Schnittke in Russia, there is very little available for the English-speaking pianist. Apart from his biography, written by Alexander Ivashkin, there are only a very small number of articles and radio talks in English.

What kind of information, then, does all this material provide us with, and to what extent is it useful to the performer of Schnittke's piano pieces?

In the case of the scores we can reframe this question as: to what extent are the scores 'self-explanatory' and do they provide the performer with enough information to make good interpretative choices? The first thing that is striking, when looking at the scores, is how conventional the notation looks, although there is nothing conventional about the music itself. Schnittke gives his piano writing a very personal colour without breaking with the rich writing tradition for this instrument. Apart from a fairly frequent use of clusters, the music is not obviously avant-garde: there is no other sign of extended technique in his solo pieces. He also uses conventional pitch and note value notations, with very few exceptions. The most significant of these exceptions is his use of wave-like lines in both staves, towards the end of the Second Piano Sonata, to indicate that the performer should improvise for four bars (see Example 6.1).

In spite of the basically conventional look of the pieces, his scores are scattered with ambiguous elements which can be seen by an inquisitive performer as small, challenging riddles. For example, Schnittke occasionally

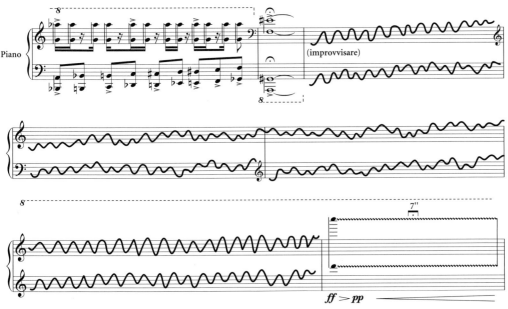

6.1 Schnittke, Piano Sonata No. 2, 3rd mvt, bars 65–71

omits time signatures and/or bar lines for a whole section of a piece. In the case of the First Piano Sonata, the whole of the first movement is metre-free. Schnittke gives the performer just a vague guideline as to how to interpret it from a rhythmical point of view by assigning specific values to most of the notes. This kind of indeterminacy suggests a feeling of freedom from the boundaries of time and space, almost a sense of 'eternity'.

We have the same lack of metrical indications in the Allegretto sections of his Prelude and Fugue. These sections contain material borrowed from early works, one of which is the opera *The Eleventh Commandment*: from it he took an element similar to the rhythm of Morse code (see Example 6.2).

6.2 Schnittke, Prelude and Fugue, Prelude, bar 11

Within the context of the opera, the Morse code element has a very clear connotation. However, once it has been transferred to the Prelude and Fugue its function becomes ambiguous. The lack of time signature makes two different rhythmic interpretations possible, each one communicating a particular mood. In one case, the passage could be counted in quavers and, therefore, the first of each group of semiquavers would have to be stressed. This would give quite a light-hearted, dance-like feel to the section. On the other hand, if you want to suggest the original meaning of the borrowed element, it would be more appropriate to count it in crotchets, therefore giving a more 'mechanical' feel to it. Without extra information we cannot be sure of the composer's intentions.

Schnittke's tempo indications at the beginning of a piece or of a section are vague, as, with one exception, he never uses metronome markings, but simply suggests the speed by using conventional Italian terminology – allegretto, lento, etc. This presumably indicates one of two things: either that the composer trusted his performer to find the appropriate speed for each piece in the given performance situation, or that Schnittke intended to fine-tune the speed in his working sessions with the performer.

As far as tempo flexibility is concerned, Schnittke has spelled out the use of rubato in just a handful of places: in all of his piano output we can find only five rubato and two recitando markings. If our approach were to take the score at face value, then the very small number of such markings might be seen as the composer's wish to encourage a strict rhythmic interpretation of his music wherever there is no clear indication of tempo flexibility. However, I find that, especially in the late piano pieces, the emotional intensity and the piano writing itself seem to suggest a more 'romantic' approach to the score. For example, there are quite a few passages in his late works that look like recitatives, although Schnittke does not mark them as such: this is the case in the second movement of the Second Piano Sonata, or in the first of the Five Aphorisms (see Example 6.3).

The way Schnittke makes use of the sustaining (right) pedal is one of the most characteristic features in his pieces. We can observe three types of pedalling. Occasionally, the pedal is used in a colouristic way, to paint an impressionistic scene, as in the Variations on a Chord, where Schnittke tries to conjure up the sound of distant bells (see Example 6.4).

At other times, its function is to sustain the bass note beyond its rhythmic value, such as we can find halfway through the fugue in the Prelude and Fugue (see Example 6.5): here, thanks to the pedal, the bass octaves are transformed into huge pillars which support the weight of all the other voices.

These two more 'mainstream' uses of the right pedal are relatively rare,

6.3a Schnittke, Piano Sonata No. 2, 2nd mvt, bars 26–7

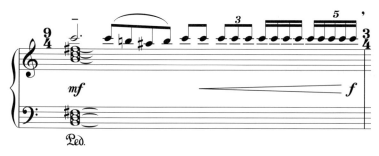

6.3b Schnittke, Five Aphorisms, 1st Aphorism, bar 7

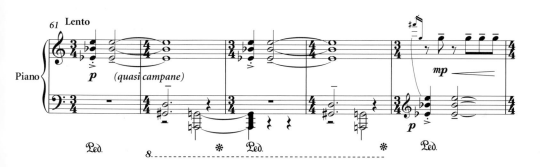

6.4 Schnittke, Variations on a Chord, bars 61– 65

6.5 Schnittke, Prelude and Fugue, Fugue, bars 84–5

especially when compared to a third type, which is, as it were, his signature pedalling. These pedal markings are long, often lasting for more than two bars, without any changes to 'clean' the sound, creating an eerie atmosphere which gives an otherworldly feel to his music. A clear example of such pedalling is at the end of the first movement of the Second Piano Sonata. Here, the opening theme reappears distorted by the pedalling and the change of register, in a ghostly memory of the beginning of the piece.

Schnittke is mostly very specific with his pedal markings and it can, therefore, be disconcerting when we find whole sections without any pedal markings at all. For example, in Improvisation and Fugue, Schnittke writes *senza pedale* at the beginning of the fugue. In my opinion, this is to ensure that the sympathetic resonance, created by holding down a long silent cluster in the left hand while playing with the right, is clearly heard. However, once the cluster passage is over, Schnittke does not indicate in any way, until the final section of the fugue, that he wants the rest of the piece to be played *con pedale*. Another example is the lack of pedalling in the last two movements of the Third Piano Sonata. As far as the left (soft) pedal is concerned, Schnittke does not give us any indications at all as to whether he wants the performer to use it in his piano pieces. The scores in themselves do not provide us with enough information to be certain of Schnittke's intentions regarding the use of the two pedals. However, in order to perform the pieces it is necessary for the pianist to come to a decision in each case.

The next investigation concerns the recordings: how helpful can they be to the performer and what are their limitations? Of course, these recordings can, to a certain extent, throw light on some of the musical riddles that we can find here and there in the scores. They do provide us with a possible interpretative version of the pieces (or in the case of the Second Piano Sonata with two versions) given by wonderful pianists who worked closely with Schnittke and who, we can assume, have had first-hand information about the intentions of the composer. However, they also raise new questions, especially when, as in the case of the Second Piano Sonata, we are faced with contrasting versions. Let us take, for example, the end of the last movement of this sonata. In the last page, at the end of the climax (bars 76–7), we have a passage with two low bass notes repeated twelve times. For some reason, Schnittke has marked here an *ossia* with only seven strokes instead of twelve. How can we justify choosing one version over the other? If we rely on the recordings for guidance, we will not find much help in this particular case: Irina Schnittke plays twelve strokes, whereas Boris Berman plays only seven.

Another example would be the development in the first movement of the same sonata. The score here does not show any changes of speed, and therefore it is surprising to hear in Irina Schnittke's version a clear slowing down of the initial tempo the closer we get to the climax of the section. Once again, we can only speculate as to whether this interpretation is reflecting the composer's intentions. The fact is that in Boris Berman's recording there is no such change of speed.

As far as all the other pieces are concerned, there is one obvious limitation of the recordings, which is that we can hear only one possible interpretative solution of the pieces, since they have only been recorded by one artist. Also, it is necessary to look for further information, to find out how much in them is the result of Schnittke's direct collaboration with the performer, and how much is Berman's personal view on how the pieces should be interpreted or the result of his performing style.

So how helpful is the available extra-musical information in providing us with satisfactory answers which neither the scores nor the recordings can give us? Any pianist seeking to know more about Schnittke and his piano works will certainly be fascinated by the account of Schnittke as a piano student: in spite of having started his official piano studies quite late (he was already 14) he quickly reached a level of mastery which allowed him to perform some of the great masterpieces in the piano repertoire, such as Rachmaninov's Second Piano Concerto and Schumann's Second Piano Sonata. We would expect his years as a piano student to have created a special bond between him and this instrument. Schnittke, however, never considered himself to be a 'proper' pianist. When discussing his relationship with the instrument in an interview about his Second Piano Sonata, he said: 'I'm no pianist and have played the piano only rarely or as an accompanist, so that I lack a well-developed relationship to the keyboard. Little by little, however, I stopped thinking in terms of keys, passage-work and pedallings and concentrated instead on the actual content of what I was writing' (Köchel n.d.). This statement can certainly explain why quite a lot of Schnittke's piano writing is not idiomatic. I believe that most of the technical difficulties in his pieces are the result of his awkward relationship with the instrument: the most difficult passages are tricky because they feel 'unpianistic', as they do not lie well under the hand.

Information about the relationship between Schnittke and his performers provides the most interesting extra-musical material. Schnittke would work very closely with his performers, not only before the actual performance of one of his pieces, but even before the piece had been composed. In a revealing talk for BBC Radio (McBurney 1990), Gerard McBurney described how Schnittke's writing for string instruments would differ according to which artist the piece was composed for. For example, pieces such as the cadenza for the Beethoven Violin Concerto or the Fifth Concerto Grosso reflect Gidon Kremer's performing style, the extrovert nature of his playing, his love for drama and, as it were, musical scandal. On the other hand, Oleg Kagan was by nature more lyrical and less interested in show-off, virtuosic passages or shocking effects. In the Third Violin Concerto, written for Kagan, Schnittke tailors his writing to the violinist's particular style of playing. When writing his First Cello Concerto for Natalia Gutman Schnittke very strongly identified with her sound and phrasing. McBurney relates an amusing comment that Schnittke made on this piece: he thought that the music of the concerto was very suited to Gutman's powerful and intense playing, but he was afraid that it would sound far too simple if anyone else played it (McBurney 1990).

Schnittke dedicated most of his piano pieces to pianists he was close to: for example, the Variations on a Chord and the Second Piano Sonata were written for his wife Irina Schnittke, and the First Piano Sonata was dedicated to one of his best friends, Vladimir Feltsman. Also, he worked closely with other pianists who were passionate about his work and wanted to perform his pieces. My question is: how did these relationships influence Schnittke's piano writing? And in what way would he actually influence the interpretative choices of the performers he was working with?

At the moment, none of the available material answers these questions. Although, as we have seen earlier, there has been a certain interest in discussing the relationship between Schnittke and his performers, his piano works and the pianists he worked with have, so far, been completely ignored.

So, where should we look for the 'missing' information? I firmly believe that if we want to find some concrete evidence to help us with our interpretative questions, we need to look for it where we can get first-hand information about the intentions of the composer. In our case, that would mean going directly to the performers he worked with in his lifetime, an area of research which has not yet been explored.

I have had the opportunity to talk to one of Schnittke's performers, the pianist Boris Berman. The information that I have gathered so far has convinced me that this line of research would be very fruitful. For example, Mr Berman told me how Schnittke would make very specific comments to help his performer recreate the exact 'emotional tone' he had in mind for a piece. Schnittke would not simply stress the details of what was written in the score, but quite often he would make changes to it to help the performer achieve the desired effect. These changes would affect details such as dynamics, pedalling, length of fermatas, and so on. For some reason, which even Mr Berman could not explain, Schnittke never changed the scores in their subsequent printing. This means that the only way we can now find out more about Schnittke's comments dealing with performance issues is by asking the performers themselves.

I believe that a collection of Schnittke's comments about performance details would be an invaluable source for today's performer: it would provide us with greater insight into his relationship with the pianists he worked with, it would show us exactly what kind of performance details he was concerned with, and it would give us some concrete answers to questions of performance practice.

There is also much to be learned from investigating the tradition of piano performance in Russia, which the composer was part of in many ways: as a piano student, as a composer working with pianists formed in this tradition, and, of course, as a listener. I mentioned earlier how Schnittke would compose his pieces to reflect the performing style of a specific musician. Learning more about the style of playing of the pianists Schnittke wrote for would show us how and to what extent it shaped Schnittke's piano writing. However, I believe that a more general look at the tradition to which these pianists belong would help us understand Schnittke's piano writing even better.

The expression 'Russian piano school' or 'Russian performing tradition' is often frowned upon because it is too general, but it is none the less worth considering the common background and idiom that inform the work of the great Russian pianists. The characteristics linking these artists include a particular way to experience and think about music, an attitude to the role of the performer and some more specific elements regarding their own performance practice.

I feel very passionate about the question of Russian pianism. I have heard many great Russian pianists, each one with a very individual way of putting across the musical meaning of what they were playing. However, I have always found in their playing some common traits: warm emotional projection, drive and sincerity, to mention just a few. I believe these to be the qualities necessary in a performance, if you want to bring to life the works of any composer, no matter whether they are 'mainstream' or avant-garde compositions.

In a BBC radio interview (Alexeev 1990), Dmitri Alexeev, one of the well-known exponents of this tradition in the West, said 'it is difficult to describe in words what the characteristics of great Russian piano playing are. Generally things are different [between Western and Russian playing]. First of all [there] are the quality of sound and style of phrasing … The entire attitude to musical performance is different: it is usually more romantic, more emotional and warm'. I find it very significant that later on, when talking about the influence of two of the great names of the 'Russian piano school', Maria Yudina and Vladimir Sofronitsky, Alexeev would stress the enormous spiritual importance that they had on the later generations of pianists belonging to the same school. There is clearly fruitful research to be done in this area.

To conclude, the information available to today's English-speaking interpreter of Schnittke's piano pieces is limited. Further research into the relationship between Schnittke and his performers, and into the 'Russian piano tradition', would provide valuable information that would help performers make discerning and creative interpretative choices.

References

Alexeev, Dmitri (1990) Talk given in the interval of a BBC Proms concert, broadcast on BBC Radio 3, 27 July 1990.

Köchel, Jurgen (n.d.) Sleeve notes for *Alfred Schnittke: Chamber Works*, Sony SK53271.

McBurney, Gerard (1990) Talk given in the interval of 'Alfred Schnittke: a celebration of the Soviet composer', live from the Wigmore Hall, broadcast on BBC Radio 3, 20 February 1990.

The co-existence of tonality and dodecaphony in Schnittke's First Violin Sonata: their crystallisation within a cyclic structure

Fíona Héarún-Javakhishvili

Paper presented at Guildhall School of Music & Drama during the Seeking the Soul Schnittke Festival, London, January 2001

The circumstances surrounding the conception of Alfred Schnittke's First Violin Sonata in 1963 are complex. In order to appreciate the magnitude of the young composer's efforts, it would be advantageous to put the composition into some context from two perspectives: firstly, from that of Russian music as a whole, and secondly, from that of Schnittke's own output.

An article in 1965 by Boris Schwarz entitled 'Soviet Music since the Second World War' illustrated the grave repercussions of Stalin's cultural policies: he described those musicians whose developmental years coincided with this suppressive period, from around 1935 to 1955, as the 'lost generation' of Soviet composers (Schwarz 1965: 259). After the Second World War, the Communist Party attempted to tighten control over literature and the arts. This control culminated in the publication of the notorious Zhdanov decree of 1948, which resulted in leading composers being subjected to severe public criticism and accused of 'formalistic distortions and anti-democratic tendencies'. While it directly influenced Shostakovich and Prokofiev, it was only part of a large-scale campaign to restructure the Soviet Union's institutions and organisations: for an impressionable young composer at Moscow Conservatory, for example, the dismissal of its liberal director, Vissarion Shebalin, and the subsequent appointment of Alexander Sveshnikov, who was considered a competent 'policeman' for the party, could be considered as yet another obstacle to overcome in the creative search for an individual voice. Many composers, in their efforts to adhere to the political ideology of the time (which was frequently 'modified' anyway) were producing music that was 'dutiful and dull' (Schwarz 1965: 270): as a result of this stale conservatism, countless operas, oratorios, cantatas and programmatic symphonies were churned out to promote the party's 'achievements'. Party officials wholly rejected the influence of neoclassicism as being harmful, for it 'represented an allegedly insurmountable impact of the bourgeois West' and was completely 'alien to the spirit of the entire Soviet art' (quoted in Kholopov 1997: 4).[1]

The death of Stalin in March 1953 resulted in a marginal relaxation of political pressures in the arts. In the autumn of the same year, Schnittke began his studies at the Moscow Conservatory. Some of the most significant figures in Soviet avant-garde music were amongst his colleagues: Andrey Volkonsky (1950–4); Edison Denisov (1951–9); Rodion Shchedrin (1950–9); Roman Ledenyov (1948–58) and Alemdar Karamanov (1953–63). While shrewd censorship still existed at the conservatory in the mid-1950s, a strong undercurrent was beginning to emerge. In spite of fierce castigation by officials, the study of significant twentieth-century figures – including Stravinsky, Bartók, Messiaen and composers of the Second Viennese School – was taking place at the meetings of the Students' Association. In conversations with Shul'gin (1993: 14) in the 1960s and 1970s, Schnittke commented on how indebted young composers were to these meetings and to the rigorous promotion of new music by its head, Edison Denisov (1929–96). However, it was also a useful platform for the listening and appraisal of their own compositions. The comments and opinions of peers often differed from tutors and were very valuable in casting another perspective on their work.

With Khrushchev as the Soviet Union's new leader of the Communist Party in 1955, the necessity for political change was intensified. He wished to improve his political profile by seemingly making concessions to the artistic community. As flawed as Khrushchev's apparent liberal attitude may have been, the cultural 'thaw' between 1958 and 1964 was a very positive period for Schnittke and his colleagues at the Conservatory.[2] They were wholeheartedly grasping all the western innovations in music, satisfying their 'ever-growing thirst for knowledge' (Grigorieva 1993: 44). Schnittke was also among the young Russian composers who made personal contact with Western contemporaries such as Stockhausen, Nono, Ligeti and Boulez.

From 1962, it was obvious that the 'thaw' was gradually succumbing to a returning chill. Khrushchev declared in a speech in the same year that the Soviet authorities were 'opposed to peaceful co-existence in matters of ideology' (Schwarz 1965: 260).[3] Khrennikov urged composers not to submit to 'foreign' experimentation: 'Our young "experimenters" should realize that there is a difference between freedom of creative searchings and lack of principles' (Schwarz 1965: 279; USSR Union 1962: 11). Officials

1. From The Conference of the Soviet Musical Figures at the Central Committee of C.P.U.S. *Pravda* Press, Moscow 1948: Dmitri Kabelevsky's speech; Yuri Keldysh's speech.

2. In 1958, a public document was produced to revoke the unjustified personal criticisms contained in the 1948 decree but the principle of 'Socialist Realism' was reaffirmed. Schnittke's opinions of the 'Thaw' period at the conservatoire are recorded in a BBC documentary entitled 'Alfred Schnittke: Words Return to Music' by D. Sturrock (10 March 1990). This period coincided with Schnittke's postgraduate studies and early teaching years there.

3. From a speech made on 8 March 1963.

68

closely scrutinised Schnittke and his contemporaries: as the noncon-
formists of the time, their music was always subject to censorship. However,
the tip of an almighty iceberg had already been exposed and it was considered a real threat to the desired unquestioning acceptance of Soviet ideology. Khrennikov admitted that the 'influences of avant-garde music' had
'wormed their way into the music of some socialist countries' (Schwarz
1965: 279; USSR Union 1963: 11). The 'damage' had already been done and
to 'rectify' the matter would be practically impossible. A controversial article in 1966 by Edison Denisov entitled 'The New Technique is not a
Fashion' highlights this new generation's creative convictions: 'The young
generation of Soviet composers turned to the new techniques not at all to
follow the current "fashion" but because the bounds of the tonal system
proved too narrow to express the new ideas constantly raised by life itself'
(Denisov 1966). The names Volkonsky, Slominsky, Tischenko, Pärt,
Shchedrin, Gubaidulina, Karetnikov and Silvestrov all appeared in a foreign
publication for the first time.

The First Violin Sonata (1963), which is dedicated to friend and col-
league Mark Lubotsky, is widely perceived as being a culmination of
Schnittke's early influences. Even at this early stage of his creative career,
paradox is an essential ingredient in his music. As the title of this chapter
suggests, the potential for paradox is implied in the co-existence of tonality and dodecaphony in the sonata. It is no coincidence that two other advo-
cates of paradox, Shostakovich and Stravinsky, were significant influences
on the writing of Schnittke's First Violin Sonata. The work has a more 'contemporary' perspective in its use and treatment of serial rows, which was
definitely inspired by Alban Berg's Violin Concerto (1935). The composer's
relationship with the violin began ten years previously with two compositions about which little is known: the Fugue for Solo Violin (1953) and
Sonata for Violin and Piano in One Movement (1954). Both works were
written in his first year at the Moscow Conservatoire and were most likely
composition 'exercises' for his teacher, Evgeny Golubev. Schnittke's First
Violin Concerto in E minor (1956–7) was a direct response to
Shostakovich's First Violin Concerto Op. 77 (1947–8), which was not premiered until 1955. Like his predecessor, Schnittke preferred to emphasise
the expressive qualities of the violin rather than mere virtuosity.

In their analysis of Schnittke's First Violin Sonata, Kholopova and
Chigereva (1990: 27) liken its cyclic structure to that of Shostakovich's First
Violin Concerto. In my opinion, however, the sonata is more closely affili-
ated with the latter's Second Piano Trio in E minor, Op. 67 (1944) for the
following reasons:

- as chamber works, they share a similar degree of intimacy and intensity;

- the passacaglia movements are the spiritual cores of the works and share similar tonal ambiguity;

- both works restore balance and proportion in the final movements through the use of symmetry; and

- the nature and functions of the cyclic returns in the both finales are directly comparable.

Before the cyclic implications of the sonata can be discussed at length, or a comparison between the two works can be made, it is necessary to outline the sonata's main thematic content. According to Kholopova and Chigereva, the compositional plan of Schnittke's First Violin Sonata encompasses four variations of a row series, one for each movement (Example 7.1). The work's 'serial development' is based upon the principle of internal growth: the intervals change chromatically within the framework of the tone row.

7.1a Schnittke, Violin Sonata No. 1, 1st mvt (Andante), **P1**

7.1b Schnittke, Violin Sonata No. 1, 2nd mvt (Allegretto), **P2**

7.1c Schnittke, Violin Sonata No. 1, 3rd mvt (Largo), **P3**

7.1d Schnittke, Violin Sonata No. 1, 4th mvt (Allegretto scherzando), **P4**

During the course of this chapter, I will present an elaboration of this analysis by outlining:

- the inherent qualities of each row series and how they are utilised within each individual movement;

- the interrelationship of the rows from movement to movement; and

- the functions of the 'serial expansion' within the sonata's cyclic structure.

In the opening Andante movement, the row, labelled **P1** (see Example 7.1a), is presented using the most basic serial techniques: **P1** and its retrograde version **R1** are treated harmonically and melodically by both instruments. As illustrated in Example 7.2a, the ascending pitches 1–5 consist of overlapping diminished and augmented triads. These are followed by descending pitches 5–8, which form a diminished 7th chord. The ascending pitches 8–12 also consist of overlapping diminished and augmented triads (but in reverse order). **P1** has 'symmetrical' qualities inherent in its construction. If one isolates the pitches that occur when the row's shape changes direction (i.e. pitches 1, 5, 8 and 12), one observes that they operate in pairs: pitches 1 and 8 (C and F) form one pair and pitches 5 and 12 (D and G) another. While the importance of the interval of a third, major and minor, is obvious within **P1**, the above also highlights the use of the perfect fourth (implying a type of 'perfect cadence').

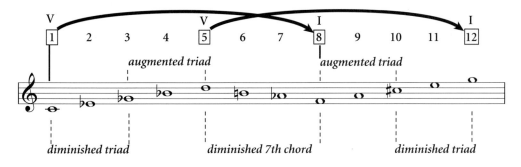

7.1a   Schnittke, Violin Sonata No. 1, 1st mvt (Andante), **P1**

In the second movement, Allegretto, the triadic nature of the second row, labelled **P2** (see Example 7.2b), is used extensively: the main thematic material (motifs **a** to **c**, which are fragments of the row) is derived from it. The influence of Berg's Violin Concerto is especially apparent in this movement: Schnittke quotes a fragment of Berg's row in bar 120 and then creates a musical allusion attributed to him. Additionally, Schnittke's intentions in the construction of **P2** are documented in a collection of conversations with Dmitri Shul'gin (1993: 25). He acknowledges Stravinsky's influence in this composition: he concerns himself with the asymmetrical shape of the row, which consists of what he calls two 'plait' ostinati – a chromatic formula

71

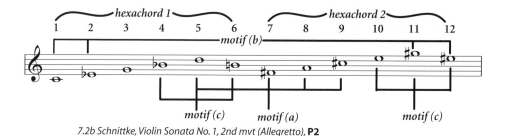

7.2b Schnittke, Violin Sonata No. 1, 2nd mvt (Allegretto), **P2**

with an intrinsic rotational quality. **P2** can also be divided into two equal halves – the second hexachord is a transposition of the first. It is noteworthy to observe the predominant existence of overlapping minor triads in **P2**: pitches 1–3, 3–5, 5–7 (descending in its second inversion), 7–9 and 9–11.

In the following movement, Largo, the third row, labelled **P3** (see Example 7.2c), has two dimensions. Firstly, **P3** provides the basic chord progression of the passacaglia, which is enhanced on each repetition. The first three chords of the progression begin conventionally as part of the cycle of fifths: C → G → D majors. However, it then digresses to F♯ major and a new cycle of fifths commences: F♯ → C♯ → G♯ majors. The G♯-major chord is obscured by the inclusion of an A in the bass (a major 7th interval). An unexpected C♯-minor chord follows it with yet another major 7th and a delayed A. The implications of this chord progression will be discussed later in the chapter. A melodic line is also incorporated within the ostinato: C → B → D → C♯ → E♯ → D♯ → C. The first four notes are a transposition (up one semitone) of the B-A-C-H motif.

The row of the final movement, **P4** (see Example 7.2d), can be divided into four separate microforms, which is what Luigi Nono termed '*quattro in uno*' (four-in-one). It encompasses the four different triads that are found in Western music: major, minor, augmented and diminished. On a more fundamental level, I feel the motif **x**, which is also the first five notes of the row, has a significant role to play in the movement's inbuilt duality between the major and the minor third. It appears many times throughout the main part of the movement in transposed forms.

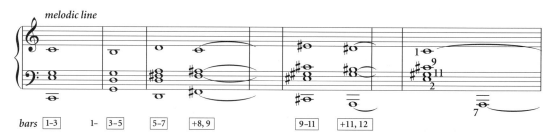

7.2c Schnittke, Violin Sonata No. 1, 3rd mvt (Largo), the vertical use of **P3** *to create the chord progression for the 'passacaglia' line*

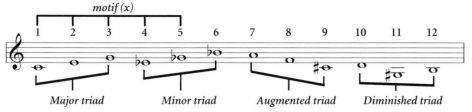

7.2d Schnittke, Violin Sonata No. 1, 4th mvt (Allegretto scherzando)

In her analysis of the First Violin Sonata (Kholopova and Chigereva 1990: 27), Kholopova draws parallels between it and Bartók's Music for Strings, Percussion and Celesta (1936). She describes how the main concept is developed 'from dark to light' by collating chromaticism and gradually converting it to diatonicism by the end of the sonata. While this is an attractive idea, I am not entirely convinced that the sonata's conclusion offers such a definite linear progression. On closer examination of the rows' intervallic contours and their relationships with each other, my deduction is somewhat different.

The concept of light and darkness being represented by diatonicism and chromaticism respectively originates from the Renaissance period. Chromaticism was regarded as harmonic imagery that depicted pain and tragedy – the use of twelve-tone chromaticism may be perceived as the most extreme exploitation of this imagery. Such representation was also concurrent with the musical language of Shostakovich and Schnittke. Many of their Western contemporaries perceived this concept as old-fashioned: for example, when Luigi Nono heard Schnittke's opera, *The Eleventh Commandment* (1962), during his visit to Moscow in 1963, he criticised the young composer's use of serial techniques, and dissonance in general, to represent only negative images and the adoption of a more traditional musical language to depict positive ones.

How does Schnittke 'develop' the use of the tone row? In my opinion, development occurs on two different levels: (1) through changes in intervallic relationships, and (2) through the varied use of serial techniques. Expansion occurs over the first three movements: the overlapping diminished and augmented triads of **P1** are reshaped to become minor triads in **P2**, which in turn succumb to overlapping major triads in **P3**. Therefore, the composer gradually distances himself from dodecaphony and moves closer to tonality. The meno section, which concludes the third movement, is described by Kholopova as a 'quiet culmination' (Kholopova and Chigereva 1993: 28): it appears that an external force has gently replaced the passacaglia theme with the unearthly quality of the violin's *ppp* artifical harmonics accompanied by a chain of major triads in the piano (Example 7.3).

Kholopova suggests that its contours are a modification of a Russian

73

7.3 Schnittke, Violin Sonata No. 1, 3rd mvt, meno, bars 55–60

dance called the 'Barinya'. In my opinion, a process of disintegration, in connection with tonality, starts with **P4**: instead of the overlapping triads found in the other rows, the emphasis has been shifted to segregation and the 'equality' of all types of triads within the realms of tonality (or atonality).

Schnittke's use of **P2** is more complex than **P1**. Aside from a few slight diversions from **P1**, the first movement appears to be a rudimentary exercise in serial writing – a system of composition rather than a means of expression. He restricts his use of **P1** to the horizontal and vertical forms of the basic row and to the retrograde form. With **P2**, however, his technique undergoes further development: the nature of the tone row makes the use of cyclic permutations, polyphonic writing and various transposed forms very flexible. **P3**, on the other hand, is used in a harmonic fashion and is therefore fundamentally tonal. Within the scheme of the whole movement, the use of **P4** is very brief (for only 74 bars): it is characterised by its use of cross-rhythms and abundance of transpositions. The prevailing impression is one of ambiguity and uncertainty.

Why does Schnittke combine the complexities of dodecaphony and serialism with the use of a traditional cyclic structure? Perhaps his ultimate aim is to formulate some kind of resolution or reverse the process of disintegration initiated by **P4**, in order to restore a balance. Therefore, it may be more beneficial to distance oneself from the technicalities outlined above and consider any probable symbolic meaning found in the work. The sonata's passacaglia movement may provide the necessary clarification. Kholopova describes the movement as 'an embodiment of faith in the stability of the human spirit' (Kholopova and Chigereva 1993: 28). Schnittke uses the sound symbol B-A-C-H, in a transposed form, for the first time in this sonata[4] – combined with the use of a traditional genre like the passacaglia, it underlines his respect for the tradition of Bach and Beethoven, as well as its continuation in the music of his older compatriot, Shostakovich. As stated previously, the passacaglia basslines of both the

4. The use of the B-A-C-H monogram is found in numerous works by Schnittke, including the *Glass Accordion* (1968), Violin Sonata No. 2 (1968), the Third Symphony (1981) and the Concerto Grosso No. 3 (1985).

74

7.4a Schnittke, Piano Trio in E minor, 3rd mvt, bars 1–8

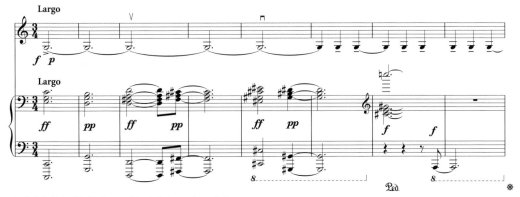

7.4b Schnittke, Violin Sonata No. 1, 3rd mvt, bars 1–8

sonata and piano trio are tonally ambiguous (see Example 7.4).

Shostakovich's ostinato consists of two tetrachords: the first, B♭–F–G–A, implies B♭ minor and the second, F♯–G–A–B, implies a modal E minor. The ostinato does not resolve until the beginning of the following movement. In Schnittke's passacaglia, the tonal strength of major chord progressions is weakened by the use of a C♯-minor chord. The co-existence of two contrasting tonal spheres, C major and C♯ minor, may be attributed to the influence of Mussorgsky in 'Two Jews' from Pictures at an Exhibition or perhaps, in a more recent context, to Volkonsky's String Quartet Op. 6 (1955). The instability of the passacaglia progression is highlighted in the contrasting dynamics of alternate chords and their placement on weaker parts of the bar. In contrast, Shostakovich's 17-bar passacaglia in the First Violin Concerto Op. 77 (1948) is firmly in F minor, coloured with Neopolitan chords.

Referring back to the contour of **P3**, after the overlapping major triads of ascending pitches 1–7, there is a dramatic descending leap of a diminished eighth (enharmonically, a major seventh) between notes 7 and 8, before further ascent is resumed. Pitches 8–12 comprise a minor triad, followed by a major third and perfect fifth (an interval occurring in a tone row for the first time in this work). In my opinion, the gradation of both dynamics and pitch has religious symbolic significance: whilst the gradation of the dynamics gradually intensifies and then subsides, the pitch register continues to ascend. Could the chain of major triads of the meno section, the 'quiet culmination', symbolise the strength of the Holy Trinity? The above evidence strengthens the argument of the passacaglia's key role within the composition: Schnittke's creative inspiration radiates outwards from its centre. This concept was not unusual for Schnittke – he also used this method in later works, such as in his Concerti Grossi Nos. 1 and 2.

Schnittke's use of the cyclic structure is an intricate network of thematic and tonal development. The integrity of the sonata's symmetry is strengthened by the linking of motivic material found within the frameworks of **P2** and **P4** in the passacaglia's adjacent movements: the central notes of motif **x** from **P4**, i.e. pitches 2–4, are a mirror image of motif **c** from **P2**. The cyclic return in the finale, which starts in bar 75, restores the work's balance. Like Shostakovich's Piano Trio, the cross-references of material in this section have a dual purpose: they are an essential part of the finale's overall intensification, as well as assuming the more common role of subsidence. The beginning of the cyclic return is marked by the combination of both **P2**'s 'plait' ostinato in the piano and an incomplete statement of the passacaglia theme in the violin. The interval of a diminished eighth is exploited to lead into a transposed version of the secondary theme of the second movement in bar 96 – it is also rhythmically adjusted to allow for its extension. The coda starts in bar 176 with an augmented version of the opening **P1** statement, which is lightly accompanied by the piano on this occasion. The open G string resonates to connect it to the partial reiteration of the passacaglia theme in bar 193 – it is stated in a high register at a fortissimo dynamic. The sonata concludes with motif **x** over a sustained C-major chord to highlight the work's inherent duality between major and minor.

In conclusion, having outlined the important characteristics of the First Violin Sonata, I hope it provides sufficient proof of how the outcome of Schnittke's skills of craftmanship results in the full integration of tonality and dodecaphony within its framework.

References

Denisov, E. (1966) 'The New Technique is not a Fashion', *Il contemporaneo* – a monthly supplement to *Rinàscita*, published by the Italian Communist Party (August).

Grigorieva, G.V. (1993) 'Stylistic Aspects of Soviet Music', *Current Musicology*, 52, pp. 44–7.

Kholopov, Y. (1997) 'Andrei Volkonsky, the initiator: a profile of his life and work', in V. Tsenova (ed.) *Underground Music from the Former USSR*, Amsterdam: Harwood, pp. 20–9.

Kholopova, V. and Chigereva, E. (1990) *Al'fred Shnitke*, Moscow: Soviet Composer.

Schwarz, B. (1965) 'Soviet Music since the Second World War', *Musical Quarterly*, 51, pp. 259–81.

Shul'gin, D. (1993) *Gody neizvestnosti Al'freda Shnitke: besedy s kompozi-torom*, Moscow: Delovaia Liga.

USSR Union of Composers (1962) *Information Bulletin*, No. 1.

USSR Union of Composers (1963) *Information Bulletin*, No. 2.

BIBLIOGRAPHY

M. Tarakanov: 'Novaya zhizn' staroy formï' [New life for an old form], *Soviet Music* (1968), no. 6, pp. 54–62

Yu. Butsko: 'Vstrechi s kamernoy muzïkoy' [Encounter with chamber music], *Soviet Music* (1970), no. 8, pp. 10–12

S. Razoryonov: 'Ob odnom muzïkal'nom vechere' [One musical evening], *Soviet Music* (1972), no. 5, pp. 30–35

V. Blinova and others: 'Obsuzhdayem simfoniyu A. Shnitke' [Discussion of Schnittke's symphony], *Soviet Music* (1974), no. 10, pp. 12–26

A. Pietrow: 'Happening w Gorkim', *RM*, xviii/8 (1974), no. 8, pp. 12–13

'Kremer and Goldsmith on Schnittke, and each other', *High Fidelity/Musical America*, xxxii/2 (1983), 46–7

V. Kholopova: 'Zum sinfonischen Denken Alfred Schnittkes: am Beispiel selner I. Sinfonie', *Sowietische Musik: Betrachtungen und Analysen* ed. H. Gerlach (Berlin, 1984), 33–42

L. Lesle: 'Komponieren in Schichten: Begegnung mit Alfred Schnittke', *NZM*, Jg. 148, nos. 7–8 (1987), pp. 29–32

V. Yerofeyev: 'Alfred Schnittke and His Music', *Soviet Scene, 1987: a Collection of Press Articles and Interviews*, ed. V. Mezhenkov (Moscow, 1987), pp. 222–9 [Russ. orig., *Sovetskaya kul'tura* (5 March 1987)]

D. Dell' Agli: 'Experimentum crucis: Begriff und Figur der Polystilistik bei Alfred Schnittke', *Komponistenportrait Alfred Schnittke: 38*. Berliner Festwochen 88 (Berlin, 1988), pp. 35–50 [programme book]; repr. in: *MusikTexte*, no.30 (1989), pp. 31–4

H. Collins Rice: 'Further Thoughts on Schnittke', *Tempo*, no. 168 (1989), pp. 12–14

I. Moody: 'The Music of Alfred Schnittke', *Tempo*, no. 168 (1989), pp. 4–11

V. Kholopova and E. Chigareva: *Alfred Schnittke* (Moscow, 1990)

S. Sawenko: 'Alfred Schnittke: 4. Concerto grosso/5. Sinfonie', *Sowjetischem Musik im Licht der Perestroika*, ed. H. Danuser, H. Gerlach and J. Köchel (Laaber, 1990), pp. 131–43

A. Ross: 'The Connoisseur of Chaos', *New Republic* (28 Sept 1992)

R. Taruskin: 'A Posteverythingist Booms', *New York Times* (2 July 1992)

J. Webb: 'Schnittke in Context', *Tempo*, no.182 (1992), pp. 19–24

A. Ivashkin, E. Restagno and E. Wilson: *Schnittke* (Turin, 1993)

Alfred Schnittke zum 60. Geburtstag: eine Festschrift (Hamburg, 1994)

P. Davis: 'Uneasy-Listening Music', *New York Times* (28 Feb 1994)

P. Griffiths: 'Schnittke's Seventh', *New Yorker* (7 March 1994)

A. Ivashkin: *Besedï s Al'fredom Shnitke* [Conversations with Schnittke] (Moscow, 1994)

F. Lemaire: *La Musique du XXe siècle en Russie* (Paris, 1994), pp. 467–72

A. Ross: 'A Shy, Frail Creator of the Wildest Music', *New York Times* (10 Feb 1994)

E. Rothstein: 'A Russian at Play Amid the Wreckage of a Lost Past', *New York Times* (8 Feb 1994)

M. Walsh: 'The Sound of Russian Fury', *Time* (28 March 1994)

A. Ivashkin: 'Shostakovich and Schnittke: the Erosion of Symphonic Syntax', *Shostakovich Studies*, ed. D. Fanning (Cambridge, 1995), pp. 254–70

G. McBurney: 'Schnittke: Life and his "Idiot"', *Opera* (1995), pp. 380–85

A. Ivashkin: *Alfred Schnittke* (London, 1996)

A. Iwaschkin, ed.: *Alfred Schnittke über das Leben und die Musik* (Munich, 1998)

A. Ivaschkin, ed.: *Schnittke Reader* (Bloomington, 1999)

DISCOGRAPHY

Stage works

Peer Gynt, ballet
Orchestra of the Royal Opera, Stockholm, conducted by Eri Klas. **BIS-CD-677/678**

Life with an Idiot, opera
Dale Duesing, Teresa Ringholz, Howard Haskin, Leonid Zimnenko, Robin Leggate, Rotterdam Philharmonic Orchestra, conducted by Mstislav Rostropovich. Sony 2 SK52495

The History of
Dr Johann Faustus, opera
Jürgen Freier, Eberhard Lorenz, Arno Raunig, Hanna Schwarz, Hamburg State Opera Chorus and Orchestra, conducted by Gerd Albrecht. RCA **09026 68413-2**

Music for films

Schnittke film music
(includes 'Agony')
USSR Cinema Symphony Orchestra, conducted by Emin Khachaturian. Olympia **OCD606**

Orchestral works

Pianissimo... for orchestra
Gothenburg Symphony Orchestra, conducted by Neeme Jarvi. **BIS-CD-427**

Symphony No. 1
Russian State Symphony Orchestra, conducted by Gennady Rozhdestvensky. Chandos **9417**

Stockholm Philharmonic Orchestra, conducted by Leif Segerstam. **BIS-CD-577**

Requiem
Soloists, Uppsala Academic Chamber Choir, Stockholm Sinfonietta, conducted by Stefan Parkman. **BIS-CD-497**

Concerto Grosso No. 1
Gidon Kremer, Tatyana Grindenko, Alfred Schnittke, harpsichord/piano, London Symphony Orchestra, conducted by Gennady Rozhdestvensky. **SIK 7-003E**; BMG Music **74321 24894 2**

Gidon Kremer, Tatyana Grindenko, Chamber Orchestra of Europe, conducted by Heinrich Schiff. Deutsche Grammophon **429 413-2**

Symphony No. 2
Soloists, State Chamber Chorus, The Leningrad Philharmonic Symphony Orchestra, conducted by Gennady Rozhdestvensky. Melodiya **SUCD 10-00063**

Symphony No. 3
The USSR Ministry of Culture Symphony Orchestra, conducted by Gennady Rozhdestvensky. Melodiya **SUCD 10-00064**

Stockholm Philharmonic Orchestra, conducted by Eri Klas. **BIS-CD-477**

Concerto Grosso No. 2
Oleg Kagan, Natalia Gutman, The USSR Ministry of Culture Symphony Orchestra, conducted by Gennady Rozhdestvensky. Melodiya **SUCD 10-00068**

Oleh Krysa, Torleif Thédéen, Malmö Symphony Orchestra, conducted by Eri Klas. **BIS-CD-567**

'Seid nüchtern und wachet'
(Faust Cantata)
Inger Blom, Mikael Bellini, Louis Devos, Ulrik Gold, Malmö Symphony Orchestra, conducted by James DePreist. **BIS-CD-437**

Symphony No. 4
Nikolai Dumtsev, Erik Kurmangaliyev, Victoria Postnikova, The USSR Ministry of Culture Chamber Choir and Symphony Orchestra, conducted by Gennady Rozhdestvensky. Melodiya **SUCD 10-00065**

Soloists, Uppsala Academic Chamber Choir, Stockholm Sinfonietta, conducted by Okko Kamu. **BIS-CD-497**

Concerto Grosso No. 3
Ronald Brautigam, Viktor Liberman, Jaap van Zweden, Royal Concertgebouw Orchestra, conducted by Riccardo Chailly. London (Decca) **430 698-2**

(K)ein Sommernachtstraum
Malmö Symphony Orchestra, conducted by Leif Segerstam. **BIS-CD-437**

Concerto, for viola and orchestra
Yury Bashmet, The USSR Ministry of Culture Symphony Orchestra conducted by Gennady Rozhdestvensky. Melodiya **SUCD 10-00068**

Yury Bashmet, London Symphony Orchestra, conducted by Mstislav Rostropovich. RCA RD 60446; BMG Music **7 4321-34894-2**

Kim Kashkashian, Saarbrücken Symphony Orchestra, conducted by D. Davis. ECM New Series **1471 437 199-2**

Quasi Una Sonata,
for violin and chamber orchestra
Gidon Kremer, Chamber Orchestra of Europe, conducted by Heinrich Schiff. Deutsche Grammophon **429 413-2**

Mark Lubotsky, English Chamber Orchestra, conducted by Mstislav Rostropovich. Sony **SK 53271**

Concerto Grosso No. 4/ *Symphony No. 5*	Royal Concertgebouw Orchestra, conducted by Riccardo Chailly. London (Decca) **430 698-2**
	Gothenburg Symphony Orchestra, conducted by Neemi Jarvi. **BIS-CD-427**
Concerto No. 2, *for cello and orchestra*	Mstislav Rostropovich, London Symphony Orchestra, conducted by Seiji Ozawa. Sony **SK 48241**
	Torleif Thédéen, Malmö Symphony Orchestra, conducted by Lev Markiz. **BIS-CD-567**
Symphony No. 7	BBC National Orchestra of Wales, conducted by Tadaaki Otaka. **BIS-CD-747**
	Russian State Symphony Orchestra, conducted by Valéry Polyansky. Chandos **9852**
Symphony No. 8	Russian State Symphony Orchestra, conducted by Valéry Polyansky. Chandos **9885**

Instrumental chamber music

Sonata No. 1, *for violin and piano*	Mark Lubotsky, Ralf Gotthoni. Undine Ode **800/2**
	Alexander Rozhdestvensky, Viktoria Postnikova. Chandos **9274**
	Christian Bergqvist, Ronald Pöntinen. **BIS-CD-364**
Sonata No. 2, *for violin and piano,* *'Quasi Una Sonata'*	Mark Lubotsky, Ralf Gotthoni. Undine Ide **800/2**
Piano Quintet	Lyudmilla Berlinsky, Borodin Quartet. Virgin Classics **VC 7 91436**
	Roland Pöntinen, Tale Quartet. **BIS-CD-547**
	Mark Lubotsky, Irina Schnittke, soloists of the 'Academia' orchestra. Sony **SK 53357**
String Trio	Gidon Kremer, Tabea Zimmermann, Heinrich Schiff. Philips **434 040-2**
	Trio Sibelius. **REV 89003**
Piano Quartet	Isabelle van Keulen, Veronika Hagen, Davis Geringas, Vadim Sakharov. Philips **434 040-2**
	The Take Quartet, Roland Pöntinen. **BIS-CD-547**

Piano music

Prelude and Fugue	Boris Berman. Chandos **9704**
Improvisation and Fugue	Tamas Vesmas. Ode Records **CDMANU1480**
Five Aphorisms	Tamas Vesmas. Ode Records **CDMANU1480**
Sonata No. 2	Irina Schnittke. Sony **SK 53271**
	Boris Berman. Chandos **9704**